HEREFORDSHIRE AND
WORCESTERSHIRE AIRFIELDS

Other areas covered in the Airfield series include:

Cambridgeshire
Cumbria
Devon & Cornwall
Dorset
Essex
Gloucestershire
Hampshire
Hertfordshire & Bedfordshire
Kent
Lancashire
Leicestershire & Rutland
Lincolnshire
Norfolk
Northamptonshire
North-East England
Nottinghamshire & Derbyshire
Oxford
Somerset
Suffolk
Surrey
Sussex
Thames Valley
Warwickshire
Wiltshire
Yorkshire

HEREFORDSHIRE AND WORCESTERSHIRE AIRFIELDS

Robin J. Brooks

COUNTRYSIDE BOOKS
NEWBURY, BERKSHIRE

First published 2006
© Robin J. Brooks 2006

COUNTRYSIDE BOOKS
3 Catherine Road
Newbury, Berkshire

To view our complete range of books,
please visit us at
www. countrysidebooks co.uk

ISBN 1 85306 984 1
EAN 978 1 85306 984 0

The cover painting is from an original by Colin Doggett
and shows a Beaufighter leaving Defford airfield
to test Airborne Interception Radar

Designed by Mon Mohan
Produced through MRM Associates Ltd, Reading
Typeset by Jean Cussons Typesetting, Diss, Norfolk
Printed by Woolnough Bookbinding Ltd., Irthlingborough

CONTENTS

ACKNOWLEDGEMENTS

I acknowledge with thanks the individuals and organisations that have assisted me with photos and personal memories during the preparation of this book. They appear in no specific order.

Bill Laws – Robert Alexander – Peter W. Jones – Margaret Wilce – Edward Dodsworth – Max Sinclair – Katharine Gaskins – Mrs L.M. Elkington – Douglas Smithson – Margaret Bradstock (for Wg Cdr H. 'Tony' Davies) – Joyce Cottam – Basil T. Shillaker – John A. Parsons – Peter W.F. Jones – Leslie Peel – Roy K. Gilmour – Ken Summerlin – Norma Farnes (for Eric Sykes) – Robert J. Collis (Lowestoft War Memorial Museum) – Trevor Watkins – Mike D. Toff – Jack Wakefield – Bob Denwood – Roy Smith – Albert Shorrock (for Defford) – Mick Wilks and Colin Jones (Defence of Worcestershire Project) – Winston G. Ramsey – Sqd Ldr Mike S. Dean, MBE – Tim Townsend – Bob Greenhill – Peter Morris – Michael Barnard (for RAF Defford sketches) – Neil Harvey – F.G.L. Phillips – Tony McVeigh – Derek Foxton – Maureen Beauchamp – E. Reed – Alex Hunter – John Rattue – Malcolm Whyatt – Norman Dolbear – Graham Evans – Dennis Williams – Wetlands Study Centre – Worcestershire Record Office – Hereford Record Office – The National Archives, Kew – RAF Museum – Imperial War Museum, London – Imperial War Museum, Duxford – Springfield Library, Maidstone – *Kent Messenger* Group Newspapers – *Evening News*, Worcester – *Berrows News* – *Hereford Times* series – *Hereford and Leominster Journal* – *The Worcester Standard*.

My special thanks go to Brian Thomas of Garway, Herefordshire for his unstinting research on my behalf. Also Mike Stimson for his collection of wartime tapes. I have tried without success to contact Glyn Warren, the author of many books on Herefordshire and Worcestershire airfields, and also Brian Kedward, author of *Angry Skies across the Vale*. Should they read this, I would be pleased to hear from them. The same applies to Richard Edeson, whose story regarding his mother's time in the Land Army came into my possession.

If I have unknowingly omitted anyone person or any organisation I offer my sincere apologies. Final thanks go to my wife Barbara for her proof reading, art work and patience skills.

MAP OF THE SECOND WORLD WAR AIRFIELDS IN HEREFORDSHIRE & WORCESTERSHIRE

HEREFORDSHIR

Shob

Credenhill

Madley

Hereford

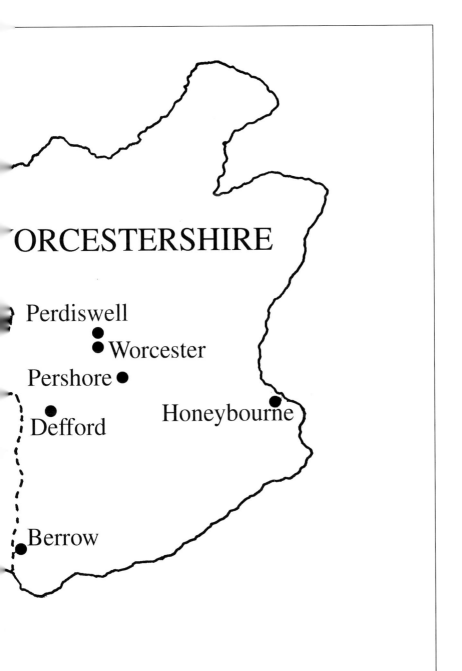

Radar operators intent on their work. (KM Group)

INTRODUCTION

Though far from the main battle front in the south-east of England, the contribution that Herefordshire and Worcestershire made to the war effort during the Second World War lay in the training of many aircrew, as well as being part of the vast manufacturing area colloquially known as the West Midlands. From factories throughout both counties came munitions, component parts for mechanised warfare and entire aircraft. Airfields in both counties were also used for training pilots, navigators, wireless operators and gunners. In the case of one particular airfield in Worcestershire, the testing of advancements in radar technology gave Britain an advantage over the enemy throughout the war.

Many aircrew gave their lives whilst serving in the various RAF commands, some of whom were trained at the airfields. Most of the young airmen of the Operational Training Units (OTUs) within the counties went on to fly with Bomber Command. By the end of the war nearly 9,000 bomber aircraft had been destroyed by enemy defences or lost to the hazards of the skies. This resulted in more than 50,000 airmen killed. They came from all parts of the Commonwealth and many died far from their homelands. The bombing campaign produced a scale of devastation never seen before, from the enemy's point of view as well as our own.

As a National Service recruit in 1960, I was stationed at RAF Credenhill to do my trade training. Apart from beginning a love affair with Herefordshire, 1 also learnt some of the history of the airfields within the region. Now some 40-odd years later and before further memories fade, I was determined to bring some of that history to print. Within these pages I hope that I have done so.

I dedicate the following to all those airmen and women, and the civilians who died or were injured during the course of the Second World War.

Robin J. Brooks

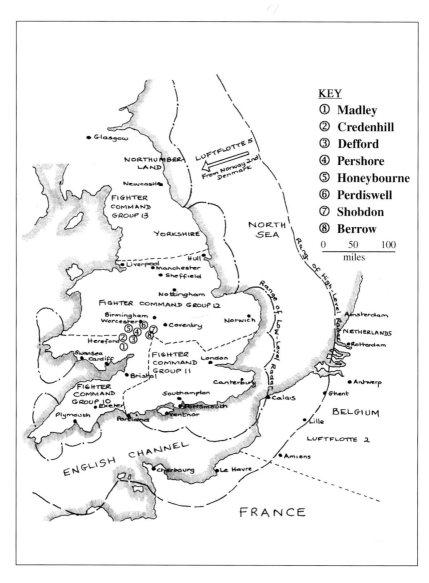

Map showing the range of the Chain Home radar coverage.

I
SETTING THE SCENE

Herefordshire and Worcestershire, situated in middle England, are deemed to be the most peaceful counties in Britain. No manufacturing smoke fills the air, despite the proximity of the West Midlands. No heavy industry makes the very earth quiver. Very little pollution contaminates the area. Yet between 1940 and 1945 the skies above them filled with all of that as well as Hitler sought to conquer the country.

Following the end of 'the war to end all wars' in 1918, Britain had slipped into a period of false delusion that such a terrible conflict would not be possible in the future. From a total of 301 airfields or landing strips in use at the end of the First World War, the number dropped to 27 service and 17 civilian airfields by 1924. When the realisation came in the mid-1930s that, once again, Germany was a distinct threat, there began the greatest civil engineering feat the United Kingdom had ever seen.

To counter this new threat, a decision was taken to once again increase the number of airfields in the U.K. The memory of the First World War still fresh in their minds, the planners initially thought that any large area of grass could be turned into an airfield. With the newer and heavier aircraft coming along, however, it was realised that larger airfields with tarmac runways and hardstandings would be needed. In 1937 the Air Ministry Works Department (AMWD) was formed to control and oversee the development of former airfields and the building of new. Some they inherited were First World War airfields upon which very little maintenance had ever been carried out. In order to overcome some of these problems, included within the organisation was the position of 'Lands Officer'. His remit was to advise on the suitability of the area for an airfield, drainage requirements and the adjustment of boundaries to ensure the proposed site was large enough to accommodate personnel and aircraft. In addition, he was tasked with determining how much work a former airfield needed in order to be brought up to the modern standard.

It was the Emergency Powers (Defence) Act, 1939 that enabled thousands of acres of farmland and countryside to be requisitioned for use. Many farmers and landowners did not want to give up their valuable land and legal wrangles were to take a considerable time to resolve. Another problem was that often highways crossed the areas needed to support an airfield. This involved much heated and time-consuming discussion with local councils and communities as to their closure. So much so that, in the end, the Secretary of State for Air himself had to intervene to move things on. Once all these problems had been settled, only then could construction begin.

The Wye Valley in the 1930s had seen a sudden rise in the number of landing strips as the idea of flight took hold with the general public. Some were situated on large areas of flat grass such as the race-courses at Hereford and at Llandrindod Wells just beyond the Wye Valley. Others were private strips for the use of avid aviators. Eastbach Court, Talgarth, Boughrood Court (which was to be used as an Emergency Landing Ground during the war), Michaelchurch, King's Acre and Kington, which was attached to a military hospital, were the most well known. Many were closed down as war approached but some, such as Hereford Racecourse, were reactivated after the war only to close at a later date. The same applied to Worcester, though there were fewer private strips compared to Hereford. The local racecourse known as Pitchcroft had seen early aviators in the persons of Colonel Samuel Cody and Gustav Hamel. During the First World War, the Royal Engineers had carried out kite and balloon experiments whilst, at nearby Norton Barracks, they had flown kites in wireless experiments. All of these early activities were to lead to the building of the permanent airfields needed to conduct future conflicts. By the late 1930s, the time left to construct them was certainly at a premium.

Nationally, 13 alphabetically coded schemes designed for different phases of building were put forward. Scheme 'A' was intended to extend the country's fighter cover northwards. In other words, fighter airfields would be built up-country for the protection of the main industrial areas there. Scheme 'B' was an updated version of 'A' whilst 'C' was for the building of bomber airfields in order to carry a projected war back to Germany. 'D' and 'E' followed similar patterns. February 1936 saw scheme 'F' in operation, which foresaw an increase in combat aircraft, namely 124 squadrons, which would require at least

14

100 new airfields. Included in this number were several small civilian airfields capable of upgrading to military standards.

Whilst the majority of these smaller airfields were to be in the south and south-east of the country, Herefordshire, Worcestershire and the West Midlands did have a few very important civilian airfields that contributed to the war effort. To mention two, Castle Bromwich had been requisitioned for use by the War Office in 1914, was again requisitioned in 1937 and became the home of No 14 ERFTS. It also became a major aircraft factory and during its time more than 11,000 Spitfires and 300 Lancasters were built there. Likewise, Elmdon was requisitioned in 1939 and was used as a flying training school and for the testing of Stirling and Lancaster bombers. Elmdon is now, of course, Birmingham International Airport.

In Herefordshire and Worcestershire, the expansion scheme did not reach its peak until 1939/40. Being far from the main area of battle in the south-east and east of England, they were always intended to be areas used for the training of aircrew. Of the seven airfields within the boundaries of the two counties, Pershore and Honeybourne were to become major Operational Training Units (OTUs) whilst Madley was to become a signals school to train aircrew wireless operators. Shobdon and Berrow were to train glider pilots with Worcester (Perdiswell) becoming the home of an Elementary Flying Training School. Defford was soon of huge importance in the world of

Wireless operators under training in a Dominie at Madley. (Crown)

15

The Boulton Paul Defiant, built at Wolverhampton and used for night-fighting from Worcester (Perdiswell). (MAP)

telecommunications and electronic wizardry. One particular station in Hereford, RAF Credenhill, was to become a major training base for thousands of engineering ground trades. It was devoid of any form of runway but aircraft were brought to the station on trailers to allow airmen to work on them.

Although just beyond the boundary of Worcestershire, mention must be made of the Boulton Paul aircraft factory at Wolverhampton. It was here that the Defiant was conceived, deemed the ultimate in modern fighter design. Although sporting a four-gun, power-operated turret, it had no forward firing guns. This was ultimately to be its downfall despite an encouraging beginning. Taken from front-line duties, it found a new niche as a night-fighter during 1940/41 when airborne radar was in its infancy.

Malvern, in Worcestershire, is known as 'radar country', for it was here that many early experiments in Radio Direction Finding and radar-equipped navigational aids were carried out, experiments that continue today in the same establishment. The technique of radar detection was developed in various ways in order to help the airmen who flew in our dangerous skies. Defford airfield was to play a definitive part in these flying experiments.

Awaiting the call: Luftwaffe crews relax beside their He 111. (Bundesarchiv)

This was also the scientists' war, and deep in the Herefordshire countryside another invention that would be instrumental in assisting the war effort, and radar in particular, was being perfected. Sir Thomas Merton is today almost unheard-of, yet one of his inventions was the long persistence radar screen, a kind of cathode ray tube. Unfortunately, someone else came up with the idea a year later and won the patent. The screen was created in two bungalows known as the 'Laboratories' adjoining a large property by the name of Winforton House in west Herefordshire. Purchased by Sir Thomas in 1923, it became a secret wartime base for much scientific research. Most military experts today accept that without his invention, the Battle of Britain might well have been lost.

A later discovery involved the use of a special gas which, when applied to the engine of a fighter aircraft, would increase its top speed by about 45 mph. This application was to be used to great effect during the battle with Hitler's revenge weapon, the V1 rocket. On 24 August 1944, out of 101 V1s launched against the U.K. on that day, 97 were brought down, many by fighter aircraft with gas-boosted engines. A light-reducing black paint was also perfected by Sir Thomas in the 'Laboratories'. When applied to bomber aircraft, this paint reduced the light reflected from the fuselage if caught in the beam of a searchlight to less than 1%.

Secluded as it was, Winforton House played host to many of the leading scientists of the day. Henry Tizard and Barnes Wallis were among the most frequent visitors, together with Lords Cherwell and Berkeley. Sir Thomas Merton's inventions played a major part in the defeat of Nazi Germany and Winforton House stands today as a testament to an unsung hero of scientific intelligence.

And so as the country went to war, 116 airfields were ready to take on the might of the Luftwaffe. No one knew just what the following years would bring but like the rest of the United Kingdom, Herefordshire and Worcestershire were ready to play their part. Let the last words come from Winston Churchill:

'There are vast numbers who will render faithful service in this war, but whose names will never be known, whose deeds will never be recorded. This is a war of the unknown warriors.'

2
PREPARATIONS FOR WAR

In order for the expansion of the RAF to go forward at an accelerated pace, buildings on all the new and upgraded airfields were constructed to a uniform design wherever possible. Even though war was imminent, plans had to be subjected to approval by the Royal Fine Arts Commission and also the Society for the Protection of Rural England. Once given, the construction of the permanent buildings could begin.

The Control Tower

Surely the most evocative of all buildings left on the wartime airfields is the watch tower or watch office. Today, due to its American connotations, it is called the control tower.

Prior to 1939, control of aircraft movements in the RAF was non-existent. It was left to the pilot of a landing or departing aircraft to report to the duty officer for his details to be entered into the flying log. With the advent of war and the increased number of aircraft, a form of regular control had to be in place. Initially, the watch office usually consisted of a single-storey brick building but by 1941/2, when most of the airfields in these two counties were constructed, it had developed into two storeys. One of the earliest designs was the Type 518/40, which was brick-built on two storeys, with windows on three sides to give all-round viewing. Some of these had a meteorological section added at a later date and in peacetime, many had a glass Visual Control Room constructed on top of the second storey.

Inside Defford's control tower. (M.S. Dean)

Another two designs that found favour were the Type 12779/41 and Type 13726/41, both of which were again two-storey, with the addition of an outside viewing veranda stretching from the front around the two sides. The first standardised watch offices were the Fort Type 1959/34 which had a tower built upon a single-storey building and the Type 2062/34 which did not have the tower. These were built at over 40 of the expansion period airfields with many of them being modified later.

In Worcestershire, Pershore had a watch office with a meteorological section, classifying it as a Type 518/40. Post-war, a Visual Control Room was added making it a Type 5871/c/55. Honeybourne, again, had a Type 518/40, a building that is today a private house. Whether in use today, deserted or converted into living accommodation, the effect upon entering any tower still standing is one of supreme nostalgia.

Hangars

Next in importance to the control tower must be the hangar. Dating from the First World War, the more common types were the gabled front wooden sheds, later to be superseded by the Belfast wooden truss hangar. In the field it was the canvas hangar that first offered aircraft and airmen protection. There were two types, the first being the Royal Aircraft Factory hangar. Designed in 1913, it was 53 ft wide, 43 ft deep and 19 ft high at the centre. Later came the RE7 Type at 60 x 38 x 20 ft respectively which was lighter, of simpler construction and thereby more portable. These were gradually replaced by the timber-framed Bessonneau hangars, some of which have lasted to the present time.

Between the wars some thought was given to the next generation of hangars. With the increase in aircraft size, a steel construction hangar known as the Type 'F' was evolved. At the same time a design known as the Hinaidi hangar was produced, examples of which still remain at Madley in very good condition.

With the new and larger designs came the introduction of a curved roof to replace the pointed roof of the First World War hangars. The Aeroplane Shed Type 'C' was the first of a series of alphabetically-named hangars. This was covered by a series of twelve gable sections which appeared as a flat roof when viewed from a distance. Very large, it measured 150 ft wide by 300 ft long and 35 ft high and was steel framed with bricking alongside to match the other station buildings. With the advent of war, eight other types of hangar appeared for various purposes. The 'D' Type were for aircraft storage units and was built of reinforced concrete with a 150 x 150 ft floor space. 400 Bellman transportable hangars were produced between 1938 and 1940. Made of corrugated iron sheeting covering the steel framework, many examples exist today on the wartime airfields. After the Bellman came 'T' type hangars, the letter standing for 'transportable', 906 of which were erected. These were built between 1940 and 1945 by the Tees Side Bridge and Engineering Works and came in three sizes according to the type of aircraft to be hangared. Again, many of these can be seen still. There were several other types designed and developed during the expansion period – the Callender for temporary storage; the 'E', 'K' and Lamella for storage; and the 'J' Type, operational.

But surely the most numerous and best-known hangars on the wartime airfields were the Blisters, of which over 3,000 were erected.

Shobdon's T2 hangar showing the ravages of time. (Author)

Designed and made by C. Miskin and Sons, the Blister hangar proved a success for the poor ground crews who had previously had to endure servicing aircraft exposed to the elements. Earlier models had curtains at one end for protection but the ingenious airmen soon replaced these with a brick-built wall to keep out even the most ferocious winds.

Many hangars have been removed from airfield sites as they have returned to agriculture but some have found a new purpose as storage areas for farmers. Modern day airfields use Hardened Aircraft Shelters (HAS) for the protection and servicing of aircraft, but will they stand the test of time as so many of the wartime hangars have?

Buildings

The expansion plans gave the RAF its first opportunity to design and build whole airfields on a uniform basis. They included buildings that would be of character, practical and hopefully, long lasting.

Many expansion airfields had hutted accommodation and work-shops. The most familiar is the Nissen hut. A direct descendant from the accommodation of the First World War, it was designed by Colonel P. Nissen, was built in large numbers on most airfields and could be in spans of 16, 24 and 30 ft. The beginning of the war, however, saw the standard Air Ministry pre-fabricated hut *in situ*. This was largely constructed of timber and was known as the 'B' Type. With a severe shortage of timber in 1940, alternative types using less wood were developed. The Laing hut, consisting of light timber, plasterboard and felt, is among the more common huts still to be seen on the airfields. Another hut to supplement timber was the Maycrete. This was made entirely of concrete and measured 16 x 24 ft. Other designs were the Iris, Romney and Marston huts, all of them requiring very little wood.

Sommerfeld Tracking being laid at an airfield. (Royal Engineers)

SOMMERFELD TRACK

WEIGHT OF WIRE NETTING PRODUCED ON DIFFERENT MACHINES VARIES CONSIDERABLY.

QUANTITIES FOR I RUNWAY 1,000 YDS. BY 52 YDS. 1½ INS. . FOR TRANSPORT AND SHIPPING PURPOSES, INCLUDING SPARES. WEIGHTS ARE APPROXIMATE ONLY.

MATERIAL	SIZE OF BUNDLES			WT PER BUNDLE			NO. OF BUNDLES REQ'D	TOTAL WEIGHT				APPROX. TOTAL CUB. FT.
	LONG	WIDE	DEEP	CWT	QRS	LBS		TONS	CWT.	QRS.	LBS.	
STIFFENED NETTING ROLLS 25 YD.	11-6 *	1-9 (ROUND)	1-9	5 (SEE NOTE ABOVE)	2	14	600	168	15	0	0	15,600
BARS, LINKING ▬ BUNDLES OF 10	15-0	--3½	--2½	2	2	0	330	41	5	0	0	332
FISHPLATES ▬ BUNDLES OF 50	1-8	--4¾	--3½	—	2	22	66	2	5	3	24	13
2FT PICKETS BUNDLES OF 10	2-3	--6¾	--3½	—	1	27	130	3	3	3	10	48
3FT. PICKETS BUNDLES OF 10	3-3	--6½	--3½	—	2	26½	130	4	15	3	1	67
*INCLUDING ALLOWANCE OF 11" FOR "SPREAD".							TOTAL	220	5	2	7	16,060

QUANTITIES SUPPLIED FOR RUNWAYS, INCLUDING SPARES

COMPONENTS	FOR A RUNWAY 'L' ROLLS IN LENGTH BY 'W' ROLLS IN WIDTH EACH ROLL IS 25 YDS. BY ABOUT 3½ YDS. WIDE. AREA .86·8 SQ. YDS. (AS LAID)	RUNWAY 1,000 YDS. BY 52 YDS. 1½ (STANDARD)
STIFFENED NETTING ROLLS. 25 YDS. LONG	L x W	600
BARS, LINKING (M.S. ROUND — 1½ x ⅜ x 15 FT. EDGED FLATS)	5.L x (W + 1) + 3%	3,300
FISHPLATES (M.S. ROUND — 1⅛ x ¼ x 20" EDGED FLATS)	I PER BAR, LINKING	3,300
PICKETS 2 FT.	30L + 3W + 4½ %	1,300
PICKETS 3 FT.	30L + 3W + 4½ %	1,300
BUCKLES, END JOINTING	6 x L x W. ON ROLLS + 25% SEPARATELY	3,600 +900 IN BAGS

SCHEME OF LAYING

① A LINE 5 FT TO ONE SIDE OF THE CENTRE LINE FOR THE PROPOSED RUNWAY IS MARKED OUT

② A 25 YD. LENGTH OF TRACK IS UNROLLED ON ONE SIDE OF THIS LINE. (MIDDLE ROLL)

③ FURTHER 7 WIDTHS OF TRACK ARE THEN UNROLLED ON BOTH SIDES TO COMPLETE THE FULL WIDTH AND THE BARS, LINKING AND FISHPLATES ARE INSERTED.

④ THE NEXT SECTION OF 25 YDS. IS LAID IN THE SAME WAY. MEANWHILE THE FIRST SECTION IS STRAINED, PREFERABLY WITH A BULLDOZER OR OTHER HEAVY VEHICLE. THE PICKETS ARE DRIVEN IN WHILE THE SECTION IS STRETCHED TAUT.
   WITH BULLDOZERS TYPES D6, D7 & D8, FULL WIDTH OF 15 STRIPS CAN BE STRETCHED IN ONE OPERATION. WITH LIGHTER TRACTORS, FIRST PICKET CENTRE OF RUNWAY TEMPORARILY AND STRAIN FROM BOTH EDGES. AFTER EDGES ARE ANCHORED CENTRE PICKETS ARE REMOVED.

FOR ALL

STRAINING
Ⓐ HEA
Ⓑ
Ⓒ BOT
Ⓓ CHA
Ⓔ STR
FOR
PULL APP

LAY TRACK IN V FORMATI

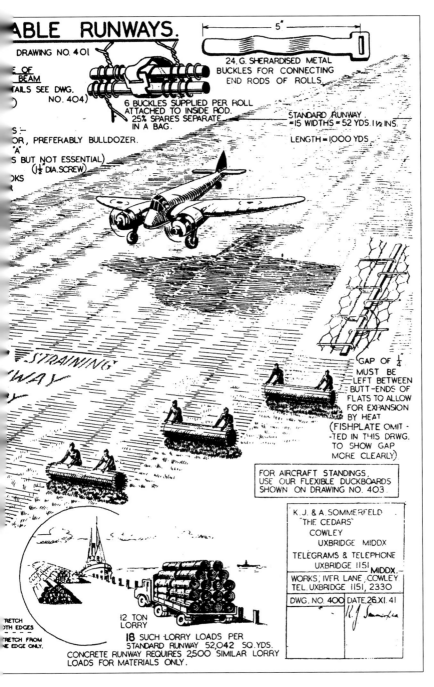

ABLE RUNWAYS.

DRAWING NO. 401

E OF
BEAM
AILS SEE DWG.
NO. 404)

S :-
OR, PREFERABLY BULLDOZER.

S BUT NOT ESSENTIAL)
($1\frac{1}{2}$ DIA.SCREW)

OKS

5"

24. G. SHERARDISED METAL
BUCKLES FOR CONNECTING
END RODS OF ROLLS.

6 BUCKLES SUPPLIED PER ROLL
ATTACHED TO INSIDE ROD.
25% SPARES SEPARATE
IN A BAG.

STANDARD RUNWAY
=15 WIDTHS = 52 YDS. 1½ INS.

LENGTH = 1000 YDS

STRAINING
WAY

GAP OF ¼"
MUST BE
LEFT BETWEEN
BUTT-ENDS OF
FLATS TO ALLOW
FOR EXPANSION
BY HEAT
(FISHPLATE OMIT-
-TED IN THIS DRWG.
TO SHOW GAP
MORE CLEARLY)

FOR AIRCRAFT STANDINGS,
USE OUR FLEXIBLE DUCKBOARDS
SHOWN ON DRAWING NO. 403.

K. J. & A. SOMMERFELD
"THE CEDARS"
COWLEY
UXBRIDGE MIDDX

TELEGRAMS & TELEPHONE
UXBRIDGE 1151 MIDDX.
WORKS; IVER LANE, COWLEY
TEL. UXBRIDGE 1151, 2330

DWG. NO. 400	DATE. 26.XI.41
	K. J. Sommerfeld

RETCH
OTH EDGES

RETCH FROM
E EDGE ONLY.

12 TON
LORRY

18 SUCH LORRY LOADS PER
STANDARD RUNWAY 52,042 SQ.YDS.
CONCRETE RUNWAY REQUIRES 2,500 SIMILAR LORRY
LOADS FOR MATERIALS ONLY.

25

When it came to permanent brick buildings, for the airmen and women, the 'H' block, having both pitched and flat roofs, became the normal accommodation. Some included an air raid shelter at one end with direct approach from the entrance hall. The sergeants' mess was another standard building designed to stand the test of time, usually consisting of a main building with adjacent wings, two storeys high. Protection against bomb attack was achieved by thickening the walls where necessary and also by the provision of a concrete roof. Of similar design, though sporting a neo-Georgian frontage, was the officers' mess. This offered messing facilities as well as accommodation. Not all airfields had this luxury, however, and for many it was a case of requisitioning one of the large country houses that seemed to abound where airfields were built.

Camouflage and Defence

Initially natural camouflage was used, i.e. the planting of trees and shrubs, together with climbing vines to cover the walls of buildings. The Directorate of Works had pointed out to the Air Staff in 1935 just how important camouflage would be in the forthcoming war. There was, however, a distinct lack of interest from the military until the prospect of war became ever more obvious. It was then that the artist, Norman Wilkinson, was given the rank of Honorary Air Commodore and told to put the camouflage of buildings on to a military footing. Just what effect one man had can be judged by the fact that in 1938 there was one camouflage officer. By 1942 there were 330!

Camouflaging runways and perimeter tracks was to prove a great problem. From the beginning it was appreciated that they had to be 'dulled' down as large areas of concrete were apt to shine. Various surface coverings were tested, with these large areas being treated with fine pre-coloured slag chippings. Airfield contractors further suggested an open-textured bituminous surfacing, which was later adopted for Aircraft Storage Unit dispersals. Certain bomber stations, however, were experimenting with large slag chippings which, whilst toning down the colour of dispersal areas etc, were sharp and thus prone to puncture aircraft tyres. They were soon discarded in favour of granulated rubber. This did prove successful until rubber became scarce and so experiments reverted back to wood chippings, this time smaller in size. In this, Pershore was to play a big part, and the experiments carried out there proved so successful that the method became standard on all runways.

The camouflage of buildings and large open areas was to prove easier. It has already been mentioned that trees and hedges were planted to give a natural camouflage. Another idea that was tried was to paint or spray 'hedge' lines over large open areas to give the impression of hedgerows and fields etc. This was fine until the typical English weather washed much of it away. Further experiments were carried out by employing certain agricultural treatments to represent field effects, a system that was later adopted. Kerbstones that had been kept pristinely white during the inter-war period were now painted different colours in order to blend in with the surrounding area.

All of this combined to make the airfields as indiscernible as possible from the air. But it did not come cheaply and by the middle of 1942, camouflage had reached its peak, with the estimated expenditure for that year alone reaching £8,750,000. The paint requirement for the same year was 27,000,000 gallons. By 1943, as the attacks on airfields began to ease, so the standard of camouflage was relaxed in certain areas. In 1944, camouflage was discontinued altogether as the enemy attacks began to peter out. Though costly, no doubt many airfields had cause to be grateful for camouflage.

When it came to airfield defences, it was the fall of France that forced rapid action. It was not until July 1940 that the General Staff headquarters of Army Southern Command issued instructions regarding a possible invasion of Britain's airfields. It concluded that airfield defence should be mainly in the hands of the army and, to a lesser degree, the RAF. Another set of instructions stated: 'Defence must consist of small groups of posts, each group forming a locality. These defended localities must be well concealed, aided by dummies and wired all round. Pillboxes and field defences should be constructed of concrete laid out so as to form a system of defences around the perimeter.' In addition to the concrete pillboxes a number of gun pits were dug. These proved distinctly unpopular with the men manning them due to the fact that they were open to the elements.

The most noticeable wartime airfield defence that can still be seen today is the surface pillbox. Various types were sited on airfields on the advice of the local defence commander, their exact positions being decided once the contractors had cleared the sites. The guns placed on these pillboxes were usually of low calibre, including such obsolete

An Oakington pillbox, some of which were built on the Worcestershire airfields. (Colin Jones)

equipment as the Lewis gun. Larger guns included the 2-pounder and the 3-inch Ack-Ack. Mobile defence was usually of local construction such as machine guns mounted in the back of, or on the top of, vans and lorries. One purpose-built mobile defence, however, was the 'Armadillo', which was equipped with a 1.5 inch gun and was issued to many airfields.

One of the most interesting pillboxes to come out of the Second World War was the Pickett/Hamilton Retractable Fort, otherwise known as the 'pop-up pillbox'. Designed by a Kentish man, Francis Pickett, it was formed essentially of two large diameter concrete pipes, one sliding within the other. The top of the inner pipe had a hatch that led into the body of the pillbox. This inner part contained the raising apparatus and also had room to accommodate two or three men. When the pillbox was in its lowered position it remained flush with the surrounding ground. Only when activated by a hand-operated hydraulic ram (or in some cases a gas bottle) did the inner section rise above the ground to allow the men to bring their arms to bear upon the

28

enemy. Once the action was over the inner pipe could be lowered back to ground level and out of range of the enemy.

These pillboxes were given top priority by the Prime Minister when he saw one demonstrated at Langley airfield. Writing to General Ismay on 12th July 1940, he commented: 'I saw these pillboxes for the first time when I visited Langley Aerodrome last week. This design appears to afford an admirable means of anti-parachute defence and it should surely be adopted. Let me have a plan.' In the end, most airfields had one or two installed but whilst a good idea in principle, they were doomed to failure in practice with problems of flooding and difficulties with the raising apparatus. By June 1941, a total of 170 had been installed at 59 airfields. However, by the time it was realised they were virtually useless, 335 had been sited. Many remain on the wartime airfields today for historians to discover.

Another good idea which turned out to be a failure was the Parachute and Cable (PAC) system which was again for the defence of the airfields and intended to bring down enemy aircraft. Rockets fired from a tube would reach a height of around 2,000 ft when two parachutes would be automatically deployed. The larger would carry

A guard post remains at RAF Worcester (Perdiswell). (M. Jones)

away the rocket case whilst the smaller had a 1,000 ft length of cable attached to it. This would automatically unreel and contained a small explosive mine on the end. It was hoped that the cable would catch on any part of an enemy aircraft and drag the mine up to the aircraft with the desired result. Both this and the Pickett/Hamilton Turret were wild ideas formulated for a country that was badly prepared for war.

A further aspect of airfield defence was the laying of pipe mines. When activated these were intended to blow up the runways whether grass or concrete, thus denying the enemy use of the airfield should he invade. The two main methods of airfield denial were the Canadian Pipe Mine System and the Mole Plough System. It was the former that came to be used on airfields with hard runways and consisted of a series of steel pipes buried in the concrete alongside the runway. These were then packed with explosive and could be detonated from a single point if the need arose. The Mole Plough System was a series of explosive-packed rubber strips that could be laid in furrows on a grass airfield and covered over. Whilst the laying of either system is not recorded for the two counties covered in this book, more than 20 airfields in the country were equipped with them. Yet again, they were never used in anger and today many are coming to light in a dangerous condition.

Decoys

In the war decoys were provided for a range of targets but for the purpose of this chapter we will look at the airfield and city decoys. These particular forms of camouflage, for that is what they were, were first mentioned at the Air Ministry in 1932. The files were then forgotten until 1937 when, with the war imminent, Alexander Korda of London Films approached the Air Ministry with the offer that his staff at Denham might be formed into a defence unit such as the Home Guard, a searchlight crew, etc. His offer was turned down but it did register in the minds of the ministers the fact that the studio expertise in making film sets could be used for some sort of war service. The old files that had been packed away in 1932 were reopened as the thought of decoy airfields was resurrected. The question of their use was put to Sir Cyril Newall, the Chief of the Air Staff, who readily agreed that the

RAF should establish daytime decoy airfields complete with dummy aircraft and buildings. It was further agreed that lighting decoys should be developed for use at night.

Tenders for the construction of the dummy aircraft were issued but in late spring 1939, with the war now only months away, the prices far exceeded any budget available. The cheapest quote for a fake Whitley bomber was £377, a Fairey Battle bomber was £116 and a Hurricane £105. Thinking about the offer made previously by Alexander Korda, Gp Cpt D.P. Stevenson of the Air Ministry suggested that an approach be made to the film studios. At the same time it was decided to ask a retired Royal Engineer and former director of Works and Buildings at the Air Ministry to take up a third career by heading the decoy programme. His name was Colonel Sir John Turner and his new appointment and remit created what became known as Colonel Turner's Department.

By the time war began, very little had been done to push the programme forward. A visit to Shepperton Studios in October 1939, however, where Turner met the craftsmen of Sound City Films, did see the start of a relationship between him and Norman Loudon of Sound City. Both men were eager to see the decoy programme start and with Loudon in charge of making dummy aircraft, Colonel Turner got on with planning where and when the decoy airfields were to be established.

Initially they were to be categorised by an alphabetic system. A 'K' site was one that had dummy aircraft and buildings for day use and a 'Q' site was one which simulated airfield lighting to divert night raids. By the new year of 1940, Colonel Turner was able to report that 36 sites had been selected and that work had begun on 22 of them. They were to be manned by RAF personnel drawn mainly from the parent stations. As the work got under way, tenders for the building of dummy aircraft were further taken up by Gaumont British Films, Green Brothers Films and North Eastern Aircraft Components. The first 'K' sites were operational by January 1940. Three months later, all 36 'K' sites were commissioned and work began on the 'Q' sites. This involved laying electrical cables and connecting up lights to resemble an approach and runway lighting system. Work on the 'Q' sites gathered pace very quickly and by August 1940, 36 'K' and 56 'Q' sites were operational; 406 dummy aircraft were *in situ* with similar machine gun posts provided at some 'K' sites.

Thoughts now turned to aircraft factories, and four main manufacturing sites were considered. These were Short Brothers at

A dummy Hurricane sits on a decoy site 'somewhere' in the Midlands. (Imperial War Museum)

Rochester, de Havilland at Hatfield, Bristol Aircraft Company at Filton and for the purposes of this book, Boulton Paul at Wolverhampton. The last was to be classified as a 'QF' and 'QL' site, the last two letters indicating fire and lighting. A decoy was to be laid at Coven near Wolverhampton, together with fake lighting to indicate the Boulton Paul plant. This site and Birmingham City were to receive the first fire decoys within the area. They were known by the code-name 'Starfish'.

Once again responsibility for these sites lay with Colonel Turner. Intelligence had forecast that Birmingham was to receive an air attack on Saturday, 23rd November 1940. That afternoon saw officials from Whitehall and men from Colonel Turner's Department in the West Midlands digging trenches in which to pour the fuel/oil mixture for the Starfish burn that night. In the event the intelligence proved faulty and it was Southampton that suffered the might of the Luftwaffe and not Birmingham!

Just down the road, the Boulton Paul factory at Wolverhampton was producing the Defiant fighter. It was important that work should continue and not be hindered by enemy attacks. On 14th August the interception of German radio messages indicated that Wolverhampton was to be the target of a daylight raid. The recently installed 'QF' and 'QL' decoys at Coven were put on full alert. By mid-afternoon *Luftflotte 3* with a mixture of He 111s and Ju 88s were in the area. They saw Coven with its dummy aircraft and buildings and, mistaking it for Boulton Paul, deposited their bombs in three heavy raids on the decoy, allowing production of the fighter to continue.

That these devices were successful may be gauged by the fact that by 31st July 1941, 60 attacks had been made on 30 dummy airfields whilst only 10 were made on parent airfields. By June 1942, 'Q' sites had absorbed 375 attacks, saving many of the major genuine airfields from damage. By the end of 1941 with the intense daylight raids easing, there were only three 'K' sites left in operation. The rest had been upgraded to 'Q' sites, the number of which now stood at 112 backed up by 90 'QF's (small fires), 170 'QL's (major fires) and 164 Starfish. All the 'K' sites had been abandoned by February 1942 with the factory decoys closing down in May 1942 as the war began to go the Allies' way. Starfish was to continue for several more years protecting different cities.

The cost of the decoy programme ran into millions of pounds but the saving of lives, aircraft, buildings and plant was incalculable. Both Herefordshire and Worcestershire had decoys of some nature. Of the airfields, Defford had a 'Q' site at Longdon, Pershore a 'Q' site at Netherton, and Hereford (Madley or Credenhill) a 'QF' site at Bishopstone. Civil Starfish operated for Birmingham at Balsall, Holt End, Maxstroke, Fairfield, Bickenhill, Peopleton, Halford and Silvington, while Wolverhampton was protected at Shipley and Blakes Hall. Army decoys at Hereford were 'QF' and 'QL' sites at Holme Lacy. Civil 'QF & QL' decoys were found for Birmingham at Newton, Little Aston, Great Barr, Overgreen, Kingsbury, Maxstoke, Bickenhill, Alvechurch, Illey, Stourbridge, Uphampton, Shrawley, Ribbesford, Mappleborough, Morton Bagot, Meriden and Tile Cross. Wolverhampton had a similar site at Coven.

These were the main preparations made as the country went to war. Without such devices and inventions, damage sustained by enemy attacks would certainly have been far greater.

3
DEFFORD

Situated one mile west of Defford village and three miles to the south-west of Pershore, the site of RAF Defford gives an uninterrupted view straight across to the Malvern Hills. It became the main airfield in the country for conducting experiments in radar, together with flying tests on a range of extraordinary electronic developments that helped bring the war to a successful conclusion.

Land was requisitioned from the Croome Estate, then owned by the Earl of Coventry, for a class 'A' bomber airfield. The building of the base was a slow process. Long before it was completed the decision was made that Defford should become a satellite of nearby Pershore where No 23 Operational Training Unit (OTU) were resident, and not a major bomber airfield. Pershore was operational by April 1941, followed by Defford six months later. However, Defford was operational in name only, for even by late September the facilities for a fully manned airfield were incomplete.

Katharine Gaskins, then aged 15, had connections with Defford and Pershore having been born and brought up in the rural area between the two. 'On leaving school in 1942 with good shorthand and typing certificates,' she recalls, 'I was directed by the Labour Exchange to work in the office of the Hadsphaltic Construction Company at Defford aerodrome to "help with the war effort". We worked in crude wooden huts heated by a coke stove. The builders were mainly Irishmen who worked extremely hard in all weathers. The local constable sat in the office every Friday whilst all these men were paid in cash. As the airfield neared completion and became semi-operational, my colleagues (being older) were either called up or had to transfer to Haverfordwest. Although I had been offered a private job in Pershore, I was told I had to stay until the Defford contract ended in September 1944.'

The advance RAF party in 1941, consisting of one officer and 33 NCOs and airmen, found that as with other airfields within the area,

A fine shot of Defford taken in 1946. (G.A. Evans)

'Marble Arch', the London Gate main entrance to Croome Court and the airfield. It remains standing to this day. (G.A. Evans)

Defford's daily routine would involve a lot of walking. The sleeping accommodation for aircrew consisted of a series of wooden huts next to the main London, Midland and Scottish Railway line. The officers' mess, a Nissen hut where most of the meals were served, was at the extreme other end of the airfield. As walking across the three runways was not permitted, it was a long trek around a very muddy perimeter to get to the other buildings. Life at Defford in those early days, for some, was not too pleasant! Despite these hardships the memories still evoke a feeling that Defford, built as it was in the Vale of Evesham, could not have been in a better place.

Katharine Gaskins continues: 'my trip down Memory Lane begins at the magnificent entrance to the Earl of Coventry's Croome Court, which was affectionately known as Marble Arch to the many hundreds of airmen, WAAFs and naval personnel who passed this way whilst serving at RAF Defford during the war years. This area is only just part of the beautiful park with its wonderful trees. Created from a swamp, all the grounds and hillocks were laid out by Lancelot, alias "Capability", Brown. The transformation of part of the Croome estate into an airfield began during 1941/2 with the building of three concrete runways, several main hangars, twenty-one Blister hangars and six aircraft pens. I am not quite sure what Capability Brown would have thought of the destruction of part of the estate.'

By September 1941, a limited amount of flying was able to take place. A mobile watch office served as an airfield control unit whilst airfield defence buildings such as the battle headquarters and two Oakington pillboxes were deemed ready for use. Wellingtons of 23 OTU were now able to use the facilities for limited daylight training exercises, known as 'circuits and bumps'. It was this activity that possibly brought Defford and the surrounding area to the attention of the Luftwaffe.

December had proved a disappointing month, with bad weather hampering training. The Luftwaffe, also restricted by bad weather, initially confined much of their activity to sea mining and anti-shipping attacks in coastal waters. Later in the month, however, with a break in the weather, enemy attacks on cities in the Midlands and north-east increased. On 11th December, enemy aircraft were in the vicinity of Defford when seven high explosive (HE) bombs were dropped near Bredon, a short distance away.

The early months of 1942 were to continue in similar vein with aircraft of the OTU flying from Pershore to practise circuits and bumps. In order for these training sorties to take place, it was necessary first to obtain a good weather report. This usually involved an aircraft from the OTU going aloft to assess conditions and 18th March saw Wellington Ic X9627's attempt to carry out such a test end in tragedy. Taking off from Defford in quiet conditions at 14.15 hrs, FO D. J. Browne was seen banking to port a mile or so from the airfield, whereupon a wingtip struck a hedge, bringing the aircraft down. FO Browne suffered very bad head injuries, dying shortly after, whilst his wireless operator, Sgt J. Heslop, was treated for lacerations to his face and hands. The rest of the crew survived unhurt.

Eleven days later, Wellington Ic X9629 crashed, injuring the entire crew. The port engine failed shortly after take-off and with control lost, the pilot, PO C.H. Grant, attempted a short landing but in doing so collided with the station headquarters at 09.41 hrs. There was to be one more accident at Defford before Pershore was forced to give up its satellite. Taking off shortly after midnight on 27th April, Wellington Ic R1618 managed to clear the perimeter fence before crashing and, with a full tank of fuel, bursting into flames. Five of the crew sustained severe injuries whilst two were less seriously hurt.

Around this time rumours abounded that Defford was earmarked to become a 'hush hush' station for secret work, rumours that became fact on 14th May when the satellite was taken over by the Ministry of Aircraft Production. With the few 23 OTU personnel gone, Defford was to enter its most important phase, as an experimental station connected with the advance of radar (a new word, the letters standing for Radio Direction And Range).

The early warning of enemy aircraft approaching our shores was made possible by the sending and receiving of a radio signal. Many said that without the aid of Radio Direction Finding (RDF), as it was then known, we would not have won the Battle of Britain. This system certainly gave Fighter Command the edge over the Luftwaffe during 1940, enabling Air Chief Marshal Dowding, the AOC of Fighter Command, to deploy his aircraft strategically. Later the system became known as radar and was to become highly developed and sophisticated during the six years of the war.

The first practical proposals for the location of aircraft by radio waves had been made in 1935, with the first station in use by September of that year. The brainchild of Sir Robert Watson-Watt and his team of scientists, the apparatus consisted of a transmitter and a receiver. The energy transmitted by the former was reflected back to its starting point as a luminous response on a cathode-ray oscilloscope. In the earliest stages, 240 ft high lattice timber masts containing the

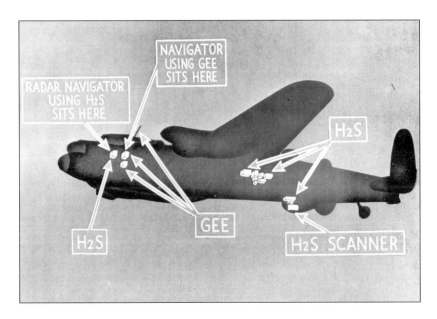

Photograph showing radar navigation aids, all tested in flights from Defford. (Imperial War Museum – ref. E(MOS)1404)

aerials were designed with the aid of civilian engineers. The construction of the first static station, however, was undertaken by the Directorate of Works and the majority of the Air Ministry Experimental Stations that followed came under their remit.

Early experiments were carried out using the BBC Empire transmitter at Daventry. Borrowing a Heyford aircraft from Farnborough, signals were bounced off the aircraft at a range of seven miles. With this success, further experiments were carried out at Bawdsey Manor near Ipswich in Suffolk, ideal for this purpose as it was a sparsely populated area with few prying eyes about. Bawdsey was also situated on the main Croydon/Europe air route, allowing signals to be bounced off unsuspecting civilian airliners.

Between 1935 and 1939, British radar scientists made tremendous strides in the technology. Eventually, the plan was to construct a chain of identical stations along the east and south-east coasts of Britain. These would become known as Chain Home (CH) stations and would mainly be manned by the RAF. Soaring 360 ft into the air, they carried fixed antennae, one for transmission, another for receiving. When war

A Chain Home radar station. (KM Group)

was declared on 3 September 1939, of the 25 Chain Home stations completed, 15 were manned and in operation. Though there was a lack of experienced personnel, the period known as the 'Phoney War' enabled many more to be fully trained by the start of the Battle of Britain, generally considered as beginning on 1 July 1940. One problem they encountered was that the Chain Home stations were unable to reliably detect aircraft flying under 3,000 ft. This was quickly solved within an incredible seven days and resulted in a different and more sophisticated form of detection known as Chain Home Low (CHL). A prototype receiver was delivered to the Foreness station at Broadstairs in Kent and was in operation immediately.

Once the war had started, the experimental station at Bawdsey was seen to be in a very exposed position and plans were put in hand to move it to Stonehaven on the Scottish coast. There, the unit became known as the Telecommunications Research Establishment (TRE), moving later to Worth Matravers in Dorset.

With the CH and CHL stations fully established, other exciting developments in the world of electronics were taking place. Ground Controlled Interception (GCI) meant a controller on the ground could direct a night-fighter aircraft to within yards of its quarry, and was operational by late 1940, while Airborne Interception (AI), a radar carried in the nose of an aircraft that would allow it to carry on 'seeing' its quarry once the ground controller had handed over, was in its early stages.

In comparison, the Germans had made no such advances. They did have an early warning system known as Freya, but this was limited in its application. The second German defensive system, known as Würzburg, was mainly intended for directing guns and searchlights and had a limited range of twelve miles. It did have some use for detecting aircraft but was nothing compared to the Chain Home stations. Thus, throughout the war, the UK was to have the edge in radar technology – with the exception of one incident.

In February 1942 it was suspected that the enemy wanted to move their two capital battleships, *Scharnhorst* and *Gneisenau*, from Brest in France to safer home waters. It transpired that the intention was to sail them through the English Channel right under the nose of the British coastal radar stations. In order to do this, the Germans had increased their jamming of these stations from their own radar station situated on the French coast. This proved so successful that both ships sailed unscathed and virtually undetected close to the Kent and Sussex coastline. When they were eventually spotted they were well clear of

A radar operator in a Chain Home radar station. (SE Newspapers)

A factory worker producing Window used to jam enemy radar. (Imperial War Museum – ref. E(MOS)1451)

the narrowest part of the Channel where ships and aircraft could have done the most damage to them.

This very effective radar jamming by the Germans caused some consternation to the Admiralty and the Air Ministry and in order to keep ahead of the enemy it was deemed necessary to find out just what system they had developed. On 27 February 1942, a successful raid was made on the Würzburg radar installation at Bruneval. This was a village twelve miles north of Le Havre with a radar station situated on top of a 400 ft high cliff. A Commando unit formed from soldiers of the Black Watch, the Seaforth Highlanders and the King's Own Scottish Borderers approached and attacked the radar station, allowing them to carry off certain equipment that would offer invaluable information to our own scientists.

With the success of the Bruneval raid, it was felt that the Germans might well retaliate and mount their own raid on the TRE in Dorset. It was therefore decided to move the TRE to Malvern, far from the battle front, and their flying unit, named the Telecommunications Flying Unit (TFU) to Defford. Between 22 and 25 May 1942, the transfer took place and Defford began its new career under the command of Gp Cpt P.J.R. King.

A German Würzburg radar scanner, on show at the Imperial War Museum, Duxford. (Author)

One of the first airmen to arrive was airframe fitter Albert Shorrock: 'In early April I and 19 others were told to get together our full kit in preparation for a move from Hurn to Defford. Boarding a Wellington, we took off and climbed to about 150 ft when the cowlings fell off the port engine. The pilot, with a shrug of his shoulders, carried on but unfortunately about five minutes later the starboard engine cowlings started flapping about in the breeze. The instruments were reading zero so he decided to return to base. We landed safely and transferred to a Lockheed Hudson and were on our way again. Our first sight of Defford was when the pilot announced, "There's your new home." Looking down all I could see was three landing strips in the middle of a vast area of utter desolation. As we came in to land, however, I discovered bulldozers, diggers, graders, rollers etc and there was mud. Lots of it, everywhere.

'I was assigned to service incoming aircraft which certainly kept us busy. There were Ansons, Oxfords, Wellingtons, Lysanders, Hurricanes and Swordfish, most of which had to be hand swung or cranked for contact in order to start. At that time we had no starter batteries. During the four years I was at Defford we equipped and maintained almost every type of operational aircraft in service during the war. Our job was top secret, no careless talk, no cameras, no diaries. We knew

The Bristol Beaufighter was used for much of the test flying from Defford. It became a potent night-fighter equipped with AI. (MAP)

ME BF110 fitted with SN2 airborne radar. This was a captured enemy aircraft sent to Britain in 1945. (Imperial War Museum – ref. CL3299)

we were something to do with radar (whatever that was) but that was all we were aware of. When the boffins dreamed up their weird and wonderful ideas and told us to "stick this here" and "stick that there", we just did it. The result was that aircraft would fly in displaying their sleek lines but when they flew out again they would be bristling with all kinds of appendages sticking out all over the place. However, in due course, I found out that we were situated in the centre of the most beautiful part of England and life did not seem so bad.'

Defford was now home to many different types of aircraft tasked with flying experimental versions of airborne radar. Although it is not within the remit of this book to deal with the technical side of the work, mention must be made of the struggles of the scientists as they developed different types of radar that were fitted to aircraft and flown on test from Defford.

The basic principle of radar is that the direction of an object is ascertained by transmitting a beam of short-wavelength (1 cm–100 cm) short-pulse radio waves and picking up the reflected beam; and its distance away by timing the journey of the radio waves (which are travelling at the speed of light) there and back. One application – the airborne radar carried by night-fighter aircraft – was further developed as a ground-scanning radar to increase the efficiency of bombers flying at night. It was not common knowledge to the public at this time that the results of bombing German targets left a lot to be desired. Bombs were being dropped miles from the designated target and with photographic evidence confirming this, morale at all levels of Bomber Command was low. With the losses of the Command reaching appalling numbers during 1942, it became imperative that its aircraft

One of the few pictures of aircraft at Defford. Two Beaufighters await their crews – note the Blister and A/C shelters in the background. (M.S. Dean)

47

were given a means of accurate target location thus reducing the number being shot down as well as giving the crews a chance of actually hitting their target.

The invention of the centimetre-wave scanning system, known as centimetric radar, came about whilst experimenting with a current system of airborne radar. Trials at Defford began with the new technology being installed in Bristol Blenheim V6000, which was flown by Geoffrey Hensby together with Bernard O'Kane. They proved it a great success, requiring just a few necessary modifications. As newer and more sophisticated versions of the system came along, the scientists began working on the principle that a transmitter could emit a directional beam of high energy impulses outwards and downwards towards the ground. Reflections of its own impulses from the ground were accepted back by the aerial and fed into a receiver, creating a map on a screen in the aircraft relating to the ground below. With this method, the contours of the ground and buildings in cities could easily be recognised.

Further advances became possible, first with a valve known as a klystron oscillator and then with the development by two scientists at Birmingham University, J.T. Randall and A.H. Boot, of the magnetron oscillator. These discoveries were to have a profound effect on the war and once again put Britain in the lead in radar technology (the magnetron is now at the centre of every household microwave cooker!). Their importance was immediately recognised by the Prime Minister, Winston Churchill, who took a great interest in the work.

Sunday, 7 June 1942 was like any other Sunday in Worcestershire. At Defford it was business as usual as the two new ground-mapping radars, one klystron based and the other magnetron based, were installed in two of the new four-engined Halifax Mk IIs. The previous months had seen a debate at government level as to how TRE should proceed with the development of this ground-mapping radar, now officially known as 'the project' (only later did it become known as H2S). Initially two tests had been carried out using both systems. Despite the magnetron giving better results, both needed to be air tested to evaluate which would be the most suitable. In the case of the magnetron-based radar, another factor worrying the government was that if it was fitted to Bomber Command aircraft, a crash in enemy territory would allow the Germans to retrieve this very secret device and copy it. Thus many ministers and high-ranking military commanders preferred to instal the more commonly known klystron-based radar into operational aircraft. The tests at Defford involving

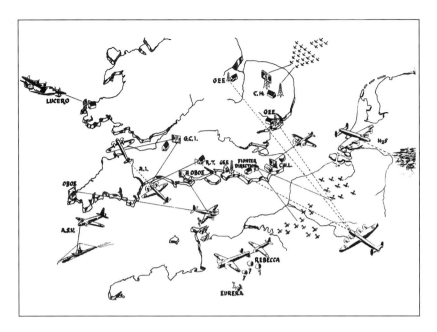

A map showing the many navigational aids originally test-flown from RAF Defford. (Imperial War Museum)

Halifax V9977 and a sister aircraft, Halifax R9490, would help to make a decision that could influence the course of the war.

By late morning on 7th June, Halifax V9977 was ready to go and a team of top scientists eagerly boarded the aircraft to test the new magnetron equipment. One of them was a genius who would undoubtedly be a household name today but for the events that were about to unfold. His name was Alan Dower Blumlein, and he worked for EMI. Before the war he had led the team whose work resulted in the BBC choosing electronic television instead of the mechanical system pioneered by John Logie Baird; he also invented stereo 20 years before anyone else would consider it.

Lifting off from the airfield at around 14.50 hrs, with a crew of two pilots, five airmen and four scientists, V9977 flew to the Welsh mountains in order to carry out certain tests with the prototype radar. With these proceeding well, V9977 was returning to Defford via the Severn Estuary when an engine failed, then suddenly burst into flames. As the fire rapidly took hold, the pilot looked desperately for a flat area of land upon which to put down. Without warning the

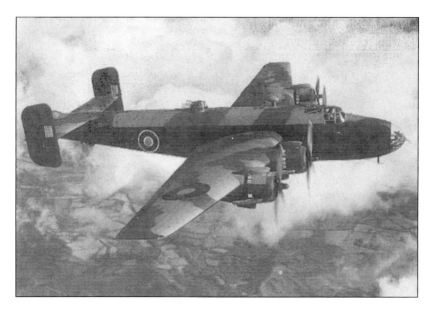

A Handley Page Halifax, similar to the one that crashed from Defford. (R. Alexander)

Halifax suddenly fell from the sky as the main spar melted through, and it crashed in a ball of fire near the River Wye at Welsh Bicknor in Herefordshire, killing all eleven on board. Those that perished were PO D.J.D. Berrington (pilot), PO A.M. Phillips (second pilot), PO C.E. Vincent, Sqd Ldr R.J. Sansom, Flt Sgt G. Miller, LAC B.D. Dear and AC B.C. Bicknell. The civilian scientists were Mr G.S. Hensby (TRE Malvern), Mr A.D. Blumlein (EMI), Mr F. Blythen (EMI) and Mr C.O. Brown.

The tragedy was subject to wartime censorship and full details of the crash did not become public knowledge until as late as 1999 when a book was published revealing the entire sad episode. In fact no official announcement was ever made and only a local paper carried any report, mentioning no names.

A telephone call to the Prime Minister told him of the loss of the aircraft and all the personnel on board. It is recorded that Churchill was devastated at the loss. Whilst sabotage was originally the official explanation for the crash, an inquiry later found the accident was due to a fitter at Defford who had failed to tighten the locknut on an inlet tappet, causing a valve to fracture.

The starboard outer engine of the Halifax II that crashed. (R. Alexander)

The accident was also a great and sad loss to Bernard Lovell (now Sir Bernard Lovell of Jodrell Bank) and the team of scientists working under him. It must have seemed like the end of the H2S project. Churchill, however, had other ideas and called the Malvern team including Lovell, to Downing Street on 3 July 1942. He is quoted as saying: 'We don't have objections in this room. I must have 200 sets by 15th October.'

To help him in this demanding target, the Prime Minister engaged the leader of the recently formed Pathfinder Force, Air Vice Marshal D.C.T. Bennett, CB, CBE, DSO. Arriving at Defford in late July and aware of what had caused the tragic accident to the Halifax, he later recorded his reaction in his book *Pathfinder* (Frederick Muller, 1958):

A Lancaster II arrives at Defford, 20th October 1945. (M. Barnard)

EAM " RAF DEFFORD ○
GHT WITH F/LT. TURNER
EATHERDALE D.F.C. ○

'A few days before my appointment to command Pathfinders, the first aircraft fitted with a test rig of this device had crashed and killed all on board. This was a sad loss and a great setback. Immediately I went down to the TRE at Great Malvern and I worked there and at RAF Defford on and off for the next few weeks. Defford had the vague idea that aeroplanes, even in wartime, had to be wrapped in cotton wool, seldom flown, but in the glorious name of "inspection" repeatedly pulled to pieces and put together again. In short, they had the most old-fashioned pre-war RAF conception of maintenance and no idea whatever of getting on with the job. The fact that I required them to test-fly at all hours of the day and night shook them to the core. Their own maintenance personnel very soon fell down on the job so I signalled to Bomber Command to let me have some men from 4 Group who were accustomed to maintaining Halifaxes. A small detachment arrived and provided the tremendous help that we needed.'

The tragedy of such a loss was to be felt for many months to come. However, although it did create an enormous gap in the research, the interest of Winston Churchill in the work ensured that it was given top priority. A signal was sent from the very top stating that if Malvern's scientists met any obstructions in their work, they were to contact Sir Robert Renwick, the Chairman of the London Electricity Supply Company who was the co-ordinator for research. He would then immediately 'phone the PM'.

Many of the pilots allocated to Defford were experienced campaigners of the Battle of Britain. They were survivors of many operations and were experts in aerial warfare. Taken off operations for rest periods, the TRE was to become their home for periods of up to six months. The station also hosted a naval section tasked with the design and research of Air to Surface Vessel Radar (ASV). Attached to No 77 Squadron, Fleet Air Arm, based at Lee-on-Solent and commanded by Lt Cdr A.H. Milward, the section used a variety of aircraft including a Barracuda, a Firefly and an Avenger. In addition work and airborne trials were carried out on the Eureka Radio Beacon system.

One marine system developed at Defford but not used in wartime was for the airborne control of interception of enemy aircraft and E-boats operating beyond the cover of our ground radar stations. The system, using a 1.5 metre wavelength, became known as Air Controlled Interception (ACI) and came about when, after the fall of France, Focke Wulf FW200 Condors, long-range, anti-shipping reconnaissance aircraft, began operating from Bordeaux. Their success

Air Vice Marshal Bennett, leader of the Pathfinders. (Imperial War Museum)

caused Winston Churchill to issue on 21 March 1941 a personal minute to the First Lord of the Admiralty and the Secretary of State for Air beginning: 'The use of aeroplanes, not only to attack our ships but also to direct the U-boats on to them, is largely responsible for our losses in the North Western Approaches. No effort to destroy the Focke Wulfs should be spared. If we could employ radar methods to find their positions and to direct long-range fighters or ship-borne aircraft to the attack, we ought to be able to inflict serious casualties.'

On 6th April the Condor problem was raised at TRE. It was agreed to fit an aircraft as an experimental flying Ground Controlled Interception (GCI) station. It was suggested that an American Liberator aircraft might be used but with only a few of the type being made available to Coastal Command, a Wellington would be an acceptable alternative. The aircraft chosen was a Mk Ic (R1629) and it was first delivered to the Royal Aircraft Establishment at Farnborough where the rotating aerial was fitted. In the end, however, the Air/Sea Interception Committee reported that the equipment required considerable technical development before service trials could take place. Thus ACI was never used in wartime, but its nature can be seen today in the Airborne Early Warning Radars such as are fitted to the current Boeing E3A AEW1.

By the middle of 1943 and with the Americans entering the war, the USAAF were becoming very interested in the performance of H2S. In May a B-17 Flying Fortress, 42-5793, flew in to Defford to be fitted with H2S. Arriving new and in a very streamlined condition, once fitted with its aerials it was described by one of the crew as 'looking like a porcupine'. So impressed were the American military with the trials that other B-17s were to arrive in due course to be fitted with the device.

Another aid to navigation, the automatic approach and landing device more commonly known as 'autopilot', was tested at Defford, as Norman Dolbear, then a Flight Sergeant, relates:

'The TFU were tasked with finding a solution to all-weather flying. The CO and the Wg Cdr Flying, F.C. Griffiths, who were both active pilots, knew the dangers of sudden weather changes. They had heard of the ideas of an American who had done a little work on a scheme but also that he had met official resistance over there because the powers did not see a pressing problem: their weather was considerably more predictable than ours. We had one of the American autopilots made by Minneapolis Honeywell which had been fitted to several B-17s and B-24s. The CO and Wg Cdr Flying had talked to the

H2S, the saviour of Bomber Command, test-flown from Defford. (Imperial War Museum)

Air Ministry and had their agreement to use an old Boeing 247D twin-engine monoplane that had arrived at Defford for the project.

'A complete Honeywell autopilot was obtained and together with all the associated equipment was fitted to the Boeing. Very thorough ground testing was followed by an air test which went very well. The next step was to carry out an auto approach. Accordingly we took off with Wg Cdr Griffiths as pilot, FO Barber looking to the signals coming in and myself keeping an eye on the autopilot. We flew over the Malvern Hills towards the Welsh Hills under autopilot control, then the auto-approach was selected. The Boeing turned gently round and settled on a course over the Malverns and towards the airfield. As the + pointer swung over, the approach beam was selected and a slow turn to port took us to face the runway. A gentle dive moved us to the end of it and at about 50 ft or so the pilot reverted to manual control for

Boeing 247D with flight and test personnel. The damage to the nose was the result of a landing accident the day before. Behind is a B-17 test aircraft. (G.A. Evans)

seconds. This was done cautiously as he then gave it back to auto and the Boeing settled down on the runway with a slightly heavier landing than with pilot control. Now was a time for glee as the trial had proved the point that an unsophisticated system such as we had worked and deserved expansion.'

The devotion to duty of the scientists is perhaps illustrated by an incident which occurred on 29 June 1942. Suffering an engine failure shortly after take-off from Defford, Wellington Z8705 flown by Flt Lt J. Bertgren, clipped the top of a ridge and crash-landed heavily on the other side. Fearing that it would burst into flames at any moment, the crew quickly left the aircraft only to realise that their passenger, the scientist Mr J.H. Bruce, had not done so. Just as two of the crew were running to the aircraft to search for him, he appeared at the hatch clutching his trial equipment. It was none too soon as the Wellington suddenly exploded about him. Leaping for his life, both he and the crew ran from the aircraft as the fire took hold. Only slight injuries were sustained by the pilot but Mr Bruce could easily have perished inside the fuselage.

Around this period of the war the Luftwaffe had changed their tactics from large scale bombing raids, on through the *'Baedeker'* period (so called because the targets were all cities listed in the *Baedeker* tourist guides), to fighter/bomber aircraft carrying out single or dual attacks. One incident occurred over the night of 30/31 July when such attacks were taking place around the West Midlands. Whilst Wolverhampton and Walsall were the centre of the raid, Junkers Ju 88A-4 (2115) belonging to 2/*Kustenfliegergruppe* 106 (Coastal Reconnaisance Wing), had strayed into Worcestershire and perhaps unknowingly, had overflown the TRE at Malvern. As it did so it was attacked by a Mosquito of No 264 Squadron flown by Sqd Ldr C.A. Cooke together with his observer/navigator PO R.E. MacPherson. The crew of the Ju88 took to their parachutes before their aircraft broke up in the air and crashed in pieces at Hornyfold Field, Malvern Wells at 02.05 hrs. Lt H. Gangl, Uffz W. Nisch, Obergefr H. Wohlers and Uffz W. Sihorsch were all taken prisoner upon landing. What is of interest is the fact that the Mosquito was equipped with a new mark of AI that was developed at Malvern and tested at Defford. The shooting down of the enemy aircraft was its first success.

The Defford station crest. (M.S. Dean)

American DC4 Skymaster at Defford, 1944

By early 1943, the three concrete runways had been completed, 01/19 being 2,000 yds long and both 14/32 and 09/27 1,439 yds long. At around the same time the TFU received its own badge. This consisted of a King's Crown enclosing a Golden Eagle with its wings flared holding a lightning flash in each claw. The motto *Fide Et Fortitudine* is translated as 'Faith and Fortitude'.

The superintendent of the TRE at Malvern during 1943 was a scientist by the name of A.P. Rowe. Very much concerned in the matter of radio counter-measures, it was he who code-named one of these developments. Known as 'Window', it consisted of strips of black paper backed on one side by aluminium foil. Cut into strips measuring about 27 cm by 2 cm and made up into bundles weighing about 1lb, these would be dropped by selected bombers at intervals during a bombing operation. The reflection from the foil threw the German radar system into confusion and was to prove a very effective method of jamming their systems. Testing of the material was conducted at Defford but its operational use was restricted in the beginning lest the enemy attempted to copy it. It was, however, used extensively during the Normandy invasion.

Wellington R1629 showing its top scanner, the world's first AWACS aircraft. (G.A. Evans)

A close up view of the AWACS scanner. (G.A. Evans)

An Avro Anson over RAF Defford's sick quarters, 15th September 1944. (M. Barnard)

H2S was to be installed in most Bomber Command aircraft from 1943 onwards, as well as in the Mosquitos of the famed Pathfinder Force commanded by Air Vice Marshal Bennett. Between 18 November 1943 and 24 March 1944, Bomber Command carried out 16 major raids on Berlin, the capital city that Goering boasted would never be bombed. The production of the Mk III H2S had resulted in a radar image giving far better definition and greater reliability. The effect of accurate bombing on Berlin was to prove devastating and was to hasten the end of the war. Mosquitos equipped with H2S were dropping marker flares directly on the main targets, allowing the heavy bombers to achieve maximum damage.

Defford eventually became the flying centre for all the scientific tests needed to further the war. The work carried out by the TRE at Malvern

Modern day Defford. (Author)

The Defford Memorial situated in Defford village. (G.A. Evans)

and the flying experiments carried out by aircraft of the TFU helped to save the lives of many aircrew. It is not possible here to list all the other systems developed at RAF Defford during the war years, but a selection must include GEE, a navigational device based on a grid system; IFF (Identification Friend or Foe) which was carried by all Allied aircraft and allowed them to prove their identity; Rebecca/Eureka, a coded homing beacon system that was invaluable for locating 'ditched' airmen; BABS, a Beam Approach system used for 'blind' landings, today known as Instrument Landing System; Oboe, an audible guidance system to help pilots fly along a given course – Mandrel, a 'noise' jammer, transmitting white noise to jam the German Freya radar systems; and Monica, a 'backward' looking radar fitted to almost the entire British bomber force which detected approaching enemy fighters appearing within about one mile. Oboe was the most accurate of wartime bombing systems, using a pair of ground stations, one called the 'Cat' which maintained the aircraft at constant range and the other known as the 'Mouse' which monitored the diminishing distance from the bomb release point and finally the release signal (bombs gone) itself.

In peacetime the experimental work carried on at Defford. During 1953 the TRE was amalgamated with the Air Defence Research and Development Establishment (based on the north site) to form the Radar Research Establishment.

In 1957 this then became the Royal Radar Establishment with the RRFU moving to nearby Pershore airfield. 1976 saw the RRE amalgamated with the Services Research and Development Establishment at Christchurch and the Services Electronics Research Laboratory at Baldock to form the Royal Signals and Radar Establishment (RSRE) to be based at Malvern. Further change came in 1991 when the MOD (Procurement Executive) establishments were divided into either the Defence Research Agency (DRA) which took over RSRE at Malvern, Defford and Pershore or the Defence Technology and Evaluation Organisation (DTEO) which included all experimental flying now at Boscombe Down and Llanbedr. Four years later the DRA and the DTEO became part of the Defence Evaluation and Research Agency (DERA). Pershore airfield is now operated by a civilian military company known as QinetiQ.

With no further military use, much of the requisitioned land was gradually returned to its owners. Part of the airfield remains, where one runway has been utilised and is now occupied by a length of rail that allows a huge satellite dish to move and track satellites in space.

Sir Bernard Lovell unveils the Defford Memorial: Graham Evans stands to the right.
(G.A. Evans)

Operated by Manchester University, it is a reflection of the great experimental work that was tested by aircraft flying from Defford.

In 1992 a memorial window to the Halifax tragedy was installed in nearby Goodrich Castle. At a service attended by Sir Bernard Lovell and personnel from the RAF and Malvern together with family members of the deceased, a plaque was dedicated in the castle chapel. The inscription reads: 'This navigational bombing aid made possible effective strategic air power whilst its maritime derivatives saved the British Isles from total isolation by submarines. Together both versions allowed the assembly of large military resources in Britain that enabled the Allies to liberate Europe in 1944/45.'

On 10 September 2002, the final piece of the Defford jigsaw was laid in place when a memorial was unveiled. The ceremony was attended by members of the RAF Defford Reunion Association, local dignitaries and Air Cadets, and civilian employees of EMI and all those companies associated with the research work.

Modern aircraft today make use of much of the equipment designed at Malvern and flown by aircraft from Defford. In December 2005 the

National Trust received full planning permission to restore the remaining wartime buildings, the Sick Quarters, which are situated at the entrance to the Landscape Park close to the 'Marble Arch'. The intention is to create a permanent visitors' centre together with exhibition space for the artefacts and memorabilia from RAF Defford. The historical buildings will remain for posterity and be a permanent reminder of those dark days in our history as well as a lasting record of the great scientific achievements carried out at Defford in the research and development of radar, the 'silent weapon that won the war'.

4

HEREFORD (CREDENHILL)

This was an airfield that had no runways and therefore no tales of heroism. Yet it did provide an essential service to the air force and thus is worthy of mention within these pages. It was also, incidentally, the station that this writer got to know intimately during his RAF training period!

The area known as Credenhill, sometimes called 'The Fort on the Hill', had a history as a military fortified position and had seen Roman and Saxon occupation. In modern times it was first used as a military complex during the First World War when the army used it as an ammunition store. With the acquisition of land under the Emergency Powers (Defence) Act 1939, Credenhill was taken over fully by the Air Ministry in 1939. It was planned from the beginning to be a hutted, not a brick-built, camp and was to receive nine Hinaidi hangars to be used for instructional purposes. Due to the hilly terrain, no plans were made to construct a runway. Aircraft that were to be used for instruction would be brought by road.

The work began in late 1938 and at one time construction of the site employed over 1,000 men to erect the wooden buildings. Though far from completed, RAF Hereford saw its first use after the fall of Dunkirk in May/June 1940. Hundreds of coaches arrived carrying the men of the British Expeditionary Force who had been rescued from the beaches. Tired and forlorn, they welcomed the safety and hospitality of Hereford after their ordeal.

In June 1940 Gp Cpt N.C. Spratt, OBE, arrived to command the now completed station. As No 11 School of Technical Training it provided a conversion course for Armourers and Fitters; trade training for Armourers; courses for promotion of Electrician 2 to Electrician 1, and of Instrument repairers to Instrument makers; a Link Trainer

Hand signal practice with a hand-held Aldis lamp. (Imperial War Museum)

maintenance course; a Mark 4 automatic control course; a camera course; and an Instructors' course.

As the Battle of Britain continued in the south of the country, the number of trainees sent to the station increased. One week in July 1940 saw 400 airmen arrive from initial training at Cranwell, in addition to a number of naval trainees. Five hundred Polish and Czech airmen helped to swell the numbers, so much so that by November, personnel strength was 75 officers, 951 permanent staff, 61 civilian instructors and 2,312 trainees.

Although building had been completed by the autumn of 1940, the particularly wet winter that year gave rise to many problems, the main one being the sparse heating in the wooden huts. With just one central coal-burning stove in the middle of each hut, many trainees were admitted to the newly built hospital with flu symptoms. Another problem was that air raid warnings at the base frequently interrupted the training schedule. The past months had seen enemy aircraft flying around the Midlands industrial areas though none had been seen directly over Hereford. Despite this, the regular wailing of the siren sent most personnel to the shelters. This was particularly irritating during the night when enemy bombers were attacking the nearby cities. In fact, it became such a nuisance that the CO posted an order stating: 'On hearing the siren, personnel are to grab some clothes and are to dive beneath their beds'! The hospital, however, did receive a number of civilians injured in the nightly raids in the West Midlands, many of whom did not survive.

In May 1941 Gp Cpt O.C. Bryson, MC, DFC, AM, arrived to command Hereford at a period of many changes in the training programme. The station was now training so many airmen in engineering trades that it did not have enough instructors or room to run some of the courses. In this case a rota system of teaching was devised whilst further wooden buildings were constructed.

March 1942 saw the arrival of Gp Cpt V.R. Feather to replace Gp Cpt Bryson. He found that Hereford now supported a staggering 6,893 personnel including 5,480 trainees. Further courses were transferred to the base including the Armourers Section of No 12 School of Technical Training from RAF Melksham. Later months were to see the School of Torpedo Maintenance transfer from Carlisle followed by 800 recruits of No 9 School of Recruit Training from Blackpool.

RAF Hereford never came to the notice of the Luftwaffe and was therefore left unscathed by bombing. It continued in the engineering training role until the cessation of hostilities.

With a diminishing requirement for certain trades, secretarial training became the core element of Hereford. The post-war period saw National Service become compulsory for most men between the ages of 18 and 21 and for these young men the courses, mainly in shorthand and typing skills, took about six weeks before they were posted to permanent stations. Yours truly was trained as a Clerk GD in 1960, one of the last to do so as National Service ended in 1962. The base continued in the secretarial training role, employing civilian instructors as well as military, and in 1969 it commenced adult training in addition to taking new boy entrants. The latter ceased in 1973 when all secretarial training was given over to regular adult airmen and women. That period also saw many Commonwealth and Foreign officers training at the Secretarial Training Squadron, as it had now become.

Hereford now became an accredited centre for NVQ courses but with an air force rapidly shrinking in the name of rationalisation, the day was fast approaching when the base would become surplus to

Electricians' Group Instructors' School, April 1942. (R. Smith)

Royal Air Force   Hereford

ADULT SECRETARIAL SQUADRON

Vivian of Heref

No. 10 TYPIST COURSE From 27-4-60 To 27-7-60.

Adult Secretarial School, Hereford. The author sits front row, third from the left. (Vivian of Hereford)

requirements. The end, however, came slowly and it was not until 1995 that RAF Hereford closed its gates. Though never an operational station, the training courses that were conducted there surely helped towards the final victory in 1945 and in peacetime filled all the secretarial needs of the Royal Air Force. Now a base for the 22nd Regiment of the Special Air Services, Hereford (Credenhill) has earned its place in RAF history.

5
HONEYBOURNE

Situated in the east of Worcestershire on the border with Warwickshire is Honeybourne. One of the largest and most active airfields in the area, it was built to a class 'A' bomber airfield pattern and eventually became home to No 24 Operational Training Unit (OTU). Far from the prying eyes of the enemy, it was to prove a first rate training unit.

Honeybourne came to the notice of the Works Department in 1940, when negotiations began with Mr Sheaf of Manor Farm, Cow Honeybourne, who farmed the land and was served with a compulsory purchase order to allow work to begin. With legal requirements satisfied, the airfield's main contractor, John Laing and Son Ltd, moved in to begin clearing and levelling the site. Once completed, drainage, water and electrical work was carried out before work on the buildings and runways began.

The main entrance to the airfield was on the western side of Rykild Street, which was also to become the technical site. In order to push the construction forward, John Laing engaged several sub-contractors for the building of the hangars and also the laying down of the runways. It was planned to construct one 'J' type and four 'T2' hangars, while the three runways were to be concrete; No 1 (05/23) was 1,400 yds x 50 yds extended to 2,400 yds whilst Nos 2 and 3 (11/29 and 17/35 respectively) were 1,100 yds x 50 yds extended to 1,450 yds. The control tower was to a 518/40 design, whilst 31 circular dispersal pads were built around the perimeter. A battle headquarters was situated on the north side of the airfield near the village of Cow Honeybourne with six Oakington pillboxes at various places around the site. Two aviation fuel dumps, each containing 72,000 gallons, were sunk into the ground, while a bomb dump, perhaps indicating the airfield's designated use, was situated in a remote area known as Saintbury Grounds.

With work continuing, the airfield finally opened in the summer of 1941. Despite its design as a bomber airfield however, it fell to a Ferry

Training Unit (FTU) to open Honeybourne's war. Part of No 44 Group, the FTU moved from Kemble to Honeybourne on 18 November 1941. Officially classified as a 'lodger unit' (i.e. before being based at a permanent station), its duty was to train crews to ferry Bristol Beauforts and Lockheed Hudsons to stated destinations. The Ferry Training Unit was broken into three flights: No 1 for general ferry training, No 2 for ferry training for the Middle East Air Force, and No 3 was allocated to No 41 Group Test Pilots' Courses.

Following the first aircraft to land an Airspeed Oxford on 18th November, an inspection was made by the Inspectorate General, Air Chief Marshal Sir E.R. Ludlow-Hewitt. This heralded the first day's flying and also the arrival of No 2828 Ground Defence Squadron of the RAF Regiment for airfield defence duties. Using Lewis and Browning machine guns, their duty was mainly airfield defence but they also guarded the aircraft in the dispersals.

A new unit was formed at the airfield when No 1425 Flight Ferry Command and Ferry Training Unit was raised for the purpose of ferrying aircraft between the UK and the Middle East. Under the command of Sqd Ldr N.M. Boffee, DFC, it was to operate the American Consolidated Liberator, a large four-engined heavy bomber converted to a passenger aircraft. Originally intended for the French Air Force, the order for the Liberators had been taken over by the RAF when France capitulated in 1940. It had first operated in the passenger role with BOAC but was later flown by RAF Ferry Command, initially to transport ferry pilots to Canada to collect and fly back the increasing numbers of American aircraft becoming available for the RAF under the Lend/Lease agreement, as well as bringing home pilots who had been trained to fly in that country. These unarmed transport Liberators were designated LB-30As, the first of which was to arrive at Honeybourne on 1 January 1942.

A satellite to Honeybourne was established at Long Marston in Warwickshire, about four miles away. Again a very large airfield built to an 'A' class pattern, it was ready for occupation by November 1941, around the same time as Honeybourne opened.

The rest of the month and December saw the units become fully functional but with bad weather (including severe falls of snow) hampering flying, only 14½ days' flying were possible. Most of the personnel were put to clearing the runways but the grass surrounding the airfield slowly became a sea of mud. Christmas that year was celebrated as well as possible. Though not yet fully functional, Honeybourne was becoming home to a variety of aircraft. From the Bristol stable came Beaufighters, Blenheims, Beauforts and even Bombays, a long obsolete aircraft. Other types to arrive at the airfield were Vickers Wellingtons, Fairey Battles and Fairey Barracudas, together with American aircraft such as Martin Marylands, North American Harvards, Curtiss Tomahawks and Lockheed Hudsons.

With a very sparse Christmas and an equally sparse New Year out of the way, operations from Honeybourne began. Inevitably accidents began to happen almost immediately. One of the worst, and the first to happen to an aircraft from the base, took place on 19 February 1942 when Lockheed Hudson V9127 crashed at 13.30 hrs in the hills near Aberystwyth. It had taken off from Honeybourne in relatively good weather to carry out a navigation exercise, but the cloud base rapidly fell. The aircraft crashed into the side of a hill, killing the Australian pilot FO D.C. Anderson, W/op Sgt R.H. Hodgson, W/op Sgt J.H. Harker and Canadian W/op Sgt B.R. Duncan. During the same month another Hudson and a Beaufighter were to crash, though with no loss of life.

With the better weather, flying hours increased allowing the despatch of more crews to their departure airfield prior to flying overseas. Mention was made of a move to a permanent station at Lyneham in Wiltshire but this was not to happen until the end of the month. Meanwhile another tragedy occurred when Hudson V8995 crashed at 17.00 hrs close to Long Stretch Farm near Honeybourne whilst returning from a training flight. The crew, Pilot FO H.D. Freams, Australian navigator Sgt J.E. Baartz, W/op Sgt T.F. Dale and W/op Sgt E. Watson were killed outright. Two days later the first party from the FTU left Honeybourne for Lyneham with the entire unit leaving on 28 March. No 1425 Flight carried on, with the first Liberator AM913 having arrived on 1 January 1942 from Prestwick. The remaining three Liberators arrived throughout January and February and commenced a series of training flights. Regular trips were made to Hurn in Dorset for maintenance and servicing until 7 April when the Flight joined the FTU at Lyneham.

It was not until 15 March 1942 that No 24 OTU arrived at Honeybourne. Assuming that the unit would receive Wellingtons as most of the other OTUs had, it came as a surprise to the airmen when they were allocated the Armstrong Whitworth Whitley instead. Designed to Air Ministry specification B.3/34 in July 1934, and chosen by the Ministry for the re-equipment of heavy bomber squadrons, they had placed an order for 80 in August 1935. It first entered service with No 10 Squadron in March 1937 and by the outbreak of war was

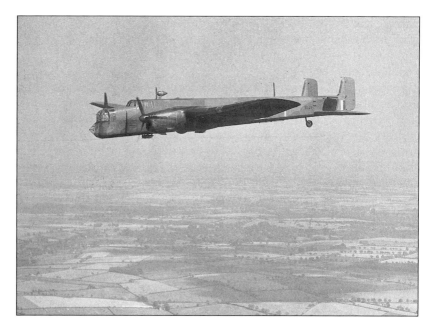

Armstrong Whitworth Whitley, the stalwart of No 24 OTU at Honeybourne. (Author)

equipping six squadrons. Five of the type initially arrived for use with 24 OTU, with the figure rising to ten by April. The latter were the newer Whitley Vs which had the fuselage extended by 15 inches, with the fins also being redesigned with a straight leading edge. In addition, the OTU had two Avro Ansons on strength for communication and navigation training.

The CO of Honeybourne, Gp Cpt E.B. Barnes, CB, AFC, had been at the station since 4 December 1941. It was his task to see the airfield through its various difficult stages of construction until it could be properly deemed a bomber airfield. This he did admirably, finally leaving on 20 April 1943 and handing the reins over to Gp Cpt A.C.P. Carver who was to see the OTU go through its most demanding period.

The task of the OTU was the training of Canadian aircrew, which began immediately the first Whitley was received. With only five aircraft at this time the unit was unable to participate in the first of the 1,000 bomber raids to Cologne over the night of 30/31 May 1942. This was the first of Air Chief Marshal Arthur Harris's 'saturation' bombing raids made on various German cities. Many OTUs were able to supply aircraft and crews but on this occasion, No 24 were left to carry on a training schedule.

As the Whitley strength increased during June and July, sadly the accident rate rose. The first serious accident, though without loss of life, occurred on 16th June when Whitley BD342 crashed onto the main runway due to a large glycol leak in one of the engines. Not so lucky were the crew of Whitley BD358 whose tragic deaths were felt throughout Honeybourne. Taking off at 15.25 hrs for a navigation exercise, the crew was made up of a screened pilot and wireless operator (aircrew teaching instructors at the OTU), four trainees and two passengers, the exercise being classified as 'over water'. At 19.55 hrs the Whitley returned having successfully carried out the exercise. On the crosswind leg prior to turning finally to land, the pilot lowered his flaps. As he did so the nose appeared to rise up. Immediately retracting the flaps, he returned the aircraft to normal flight. Turning onto his final approach, the pilot again lowered his flaps whereupon the nose pitched up once more and the aircraft stalled. It then plunged to the ground on the boundary of the airfield where it burst into flames. Those watching could only stand helplessly as the crew, FS W.T. Rushton, PO L. Rowlinson, Sgt G.E. Hibben, Sgt E.M. Taylor, Sgt A.F. Alcock RCAF, LAC H.G. Foot and AC2 J. Murray, tragically perished in the inferno. The only survivor was Sgt Harris, who was rescued from his rear turret with severe injuries. Despite the prompt arrival of the station fire service, the aircraft continued to burn for several hours. It was the first major accident involving 24 OTU since its formation.

Originally part of No 7 Group, the OTU was transferred to No 92 Group when this was formed in May 1942. Now with a full complement of aircraft, the OTU was ordered on 24th June to supply aircraft for the third of Harris's 1,000 bomber raids. This time the target was Bremen, for which 24 OTU would supply 16 aircraft.

It was the Air Ministry Directive issued to Bomber Command on 14th February 1942 that was the blueprint for the attacks on German capital cities. It included the words 'you are accordingly authorised to employ your forces without restriction' and named Essen, Duisburg, Cologne and Dusseldorf as some of the targets. Sir Arthur Harris, as he now became, was a formidable force and a great believer in strategic bombing. In order to obtain the critical number of 1,000 bombers, Harris involved most of the aircraft from Bomber Command, the

A Whitley of No 24 OTU undergoes maintenance. (Crown)

OTUs, Army Co-op Command, Training Command and Coastal Command. The 'thousand' force assembled for the Bremen raid was to include even the twin-engined light bombers of No 2 Group, these being Bostons and Mosquitos. In the end the force could only attain 960 aircraft, comprising 472 Wellingtons, 124 Halifaxes, 96 Lancasters, 69 Stirlings, 51 Blenheims, 50 Hampdens, 50 Whitleys, 24 Bostons, 20 Manchesters and 4 Mosquitos.

It fell to 'B' and 'C' Flights to be committed to the force with 'A' Flight continuing normal training. The six aircraft of 'B' Flight were under the command of Sqd Ldr L.M. Hodges whilst the ten aircraft of 'C' were under Sqd Ldr Wakefield. Early on the morning of 25th June, orders were received from group operations regarding the raid. Immediately the groundcrews began to prepare the aircraft detailed for the night's operation. Some that had been stationed at Long Marston were flown back to Honeybourne, whereupon all 16 aircraft were moved to one side of the airfield to allow arming and bombing up to commence. The load consisted of incendiaries together with two 500lb HE bombs on each aircraft. By 16.00 hrs the groundcrews had completed their tasks and the Whitleys were deemed ready. A briefing for the aircrews by the commanders followed in locked rooms where details of the target, routes to be taken, weather and possible enemy opposition were given before the men moved to their own crew rooms to continue the planning.

Once completed, every man was left to his own thoughts. Some went to the mess, others went to their rooms to lie down in silence and some sat and wrote letters home. They all came together again at 19.45 hrs when supper was served. Flasks were filled with soup, coffee or tea and a pack of sandwiches was handed out to each crew member. One and a quarter hours later, the men were on their way to the aircraft waiting at dispersals around the airfield. Climbing aboard and settling themselves in their respective positions, the rigorous check of systems began and was completed by 22.00 hrs, when the first Whitley was started up and moved onto the taxiway. Its throttles were pushed forward giving maximum power to the two 1,145hp Rolls-Royce Merlin X engines as it rumbled down the runway, lifting off at 22.15 hrs with the others following. The last Whitley became airborne at 23.06 hrs.

They found the main force formatting off the Essex coast in what had now become variable weather. As they crossed the North Sea, heavy cloud began to form. This continued as they crossed the enemy coast and carried on over Holland. Between 0.27 hrs and 02.05 hrs was their estimated time of arrival (ETA) but the Whitleys could see nothing down below as even thicker cloud, at least 9/10ths, covered the target. All that was visible were the red patches of the fires below reflecting on the clouds. Seeing a larger red patch than normal, the bomb aimers pressed their 'tits' and the bombs released. It was now time to turn and head for home but with so many aircraft in the sky over the target, the task became dangerous. Eventually the aircraft of the OTU made it back to the North Sea but even this was not easy as navigational problems continued to plague the crews.

It had been arranged that all aircraft would land at Long Marston and long before dawn, groundcrews and others were looking skywards for the first signs of returning bombers. At 05.15 hrs, the sound of aero engines heralded the first Whitley to make it back. Slowly, one after the other, eleven aircraft returned and taxied to a secure area of the airfield where the groundcrews took over. For the crews, it was a short journey to Honeybourne by bus before a debriefing in the intelligence room. Only after that did the crews finally get to bed.

Two aircraft had cause to divert. One landed safely at Coltishall in Norfolk whilst the other landed at Aldermaston in Berkshire. As the news came through that the two aircraft were safe, hopes began to rise that the other three had also landed elsewhere. However, as time went on and dawn turned to full daylight, it soon became obvious to all that 15 brave airmen would not be returning to Long Marston.

Z9441 of 'B' flight crewed by PO J.A. Preston (pilot RCAF), PO E.L. Bedford (navigator), PO W.G.W. Lapham (bomb aimer), Flt Sgt C.R. Robinson (W/AG RCAF) and Sgt A.E. Owen (AG), an all-pupil crew, was lost around 02.54 hrs, possibly shot down by an enemy night-fighter. All now lie in Becklingen War Cemetery.

Whitley BD 379 of 'C' Flight was shot down at 04.18 hrs by a flak unit on the Dutch coast. FO J.B. Monro (pilot RNZAF), FO G.R. Lind (nav RAAF), Sgt P.V. Clark (W/AG), Sgt H.H. Hudson (AG) and Flt Sgt J. Storey (observer) perished in the cold North Sea. This crew was described as a 'screened crew', meaning that they were aircrew teaching instructors at the OTU. At 04.11 hrs, the direction finding station at Sealand had intercepted an SOS signal originating from this Whitley. The station responded but nothing further was heard. It was thus presumed that the aircraft had crashed into the sea off the Frisian Islands. Some time later the bodies of Monro, Storey, Clark and Hudson were washed ashore and identified as being from BD379. Of FO Lind, no trace was ever found and he is remembered on the Air Force Runnymede Memorial as having no known grave.

The third aircraft, BD266, is also presumed to have come down in the sea off Holland. Described again as a pupil crew, Flt Sgt F.M. Cole (pilot RCAF), PO S.A. Cheeseman (nav), PO N.W. Blackford (AG) Sgt P.C. Omilianouski (W/AG RCAF) and Sgt W.P. Rixon (AG) were lost at sea. The body of Sgt Rixon was later recovered from the sea and was placed to rest in Huisoui New Military Cemetery on 23 July 1942. Since that time his remains have been exhumed and reburied in Bergen op Zoom Cemetery. His four companions, like FO Lind, are remembered on the Runnymede Memorial.

Although much of the target had been covered in cloud, on the ground at Bremen the wind had strengthened to fan what fires had been started, causing them to spread very quickly. One target successfully attacked was the Focke-Wulfe factory, the results of which suspended production of component parts for several months. Sadly however, the heaviest losses of the raid had been suffered by the OTUs of 91 Group. Out of a total of 198 aircraft drawn from the group, 23 were lost.

With the raid over, the station got back to its primary task. From a training point of view, requiring the aircraft of the OTUs to supplement the normal squadrons of Bomber Command caused many disruptions. With the Command using so many aircraft and aircrews at this period of the war, it was essential that the training of new aircrew was accelerated but despite this the units, including No 24, were called upon to participate in further Bomber Command operations.

A second large raid, on Hamburg, was to include twelve aircraft from the OTU. With the target being that much further inland, the Whitleys first flew to Horsham St Faith near Norwich to refuel. Taking off again between 22.10 hrs and 22.35 hrs, only nine managed to leave Horsham, three going unserviceable. Despite a worsening of the weather, the aircraft continued across the North Sea. A signal was received by some of the aircraft to abort the operation as they reached the halfway point, but for some reason this did not reach all the aircraft and three of the unit's Whitleys, with other aircraft, carried on and successfully bombed Hamburg. The homeward journey proved just as bad with heavy flak and changing weather but all the 24 OTU aircraft returned safely.

Another 1,000-bomber raid was planned for 29th July but was rescheduled for the 31st. Orders received from Group meant that twelve aircraft from the unit would be taking part. Groundcrews began to prepare the aircraft whilst the aircrews attended briefings behind locked doors. By 23.52 hrs the twelve aircraft were airborne and heading for the Dutch coast. Three of the Whitleys had problems on the outbound journey and had to return to Honeybourne. The other seven in company with the rest of the force found the target and successfully dropped their bombs. In all 900 tons of bombs rained down on Dusseldorf causing tremendous damage to buildings and a great loss of life.

Two aircraft from the OTU failed to return, these being Z9512 and BD347. With a loss of communication shortly after becoming airborne, Z9512 pressed on to the target and it is assumed dropped its bomb load. On the homeward leg something caused it to crash, killing four crew members. PO L.L. Syumlinski (obs RCAF), Flt Sgt W.V. Donahue (BA RCAF), Flt Sgt E.L. Styles (w/op) and Sgt E.J. Jones (AG RCAF). The pilot, PO A.W. Thompson survived the crash to become a POW. Sadly it is believed that he was eventually shot by the Gestapo.

BD347 suffered a similar fate when it was shot down by a German night-fighter and crashed near Fleurus (Hainaut). Three crew members had time to bale out, these being PO G. Silva (Pilot RAAF), Sgt D.B.R. Black (nav) and Sgt A.J. Whicher (W/AG). The remaining air gunner, Sgt W.T. Whiting, lost his life in the crash and was laid to rest in Gosselies Communal Cemetery. This was the last full scale raid in which the OTU participated. With larger aircraft now coming on stream faster than before, Bomber Command found little need to

A Whitley of 'B' Flight, No 24 OTU. (A. Thomas)

involve training units in large attacks. Another factor in the decision was the high losses sustained by the OTU aircraft.

As the unit settled down to a regular training routine, a Fairey Battle single-engined light bomber was flown to Honeybourne for target towing duties. It was rapidly replaced by two Westland Lysanders for similar duties though this number was reduced when Flt Lt J. Pestridge crashed on landing at Honeybourne, without personal injury.

Night flying exercises codenamed 'Bullseye' were frequently flown. The night of 28 August 1942 saw such an exercise when Whitley BD380 left Honeybourne for a flight over Aintree Racecourse. Around 02.00 hrs the starboard engine failed and following routine, the navigator attempted to obtain ground assistance by broadcasting 'Darky' and 'Mayday' calls. Receiving no reply, the pilot, Sgt G.H. Dodd, ordered his crew to bale out. This they did successfully with himself the last to exit the stricken aircraft. All the crew survived the bale-out with the Whitley crashing at Little Sutton in Cheshire.

The tragic incidents described in this chapter are but a few that occurred to the OTU. A full log of accidents has been produced by

Brian Kedward in his excellent book *Angry Skies Across The Vale*. Suffice to say that obsolete aircraft, bad weather and inexperienced crews contributed to the terrific and awful loss of life.

Fighter affiliation between the Whitleys and a fighter aircraft, usually an early mark of Hurricane seconded to secondary duties, was an essential part of the OTU training. This gave experience to the trainee crews, in particular the air gunners with the cine guns, and also to the fighter pilot. For the former it was a case of learning to aim at and hit enemy aircraft, while for the fighter, it was experience in approaching and hopefully destroying enemy aircraft.

Another important aspect of the training was 'nickelling', the dropping of propaganda leaflets over enemy territory. One of the first such operations carried out by No 24 was a sortie over the night of 9/10 December 1942. Five aircraft were detailed to participate with a take-off time of 18.25 hrs, carrying a quantity of F155 and F157 packages. The area for the drop was Orléans in France and all five aircraft reached it and dropped the leaflets. Bad weather plagued the return journey though all except one, EB388 flown by FO F.P. Saunders, landed safely albeit at different airfields. No contact had been made with Saunders' Whitley since take-off, which suggested that it had been lost. Due to darkness it was not possible to launch a search but next morning a land search was carried out which revealed nothing. It was later established that the aircraft had come down at Senoches near Chartres, sadly with the loss of all five crew.

Christmas 1942 was a sombre affair. Those not on essential duties were allowed leave but at Honeybourne, the many losses over the past six months resulted in a worrying time for all aircrew. They were still battling on with the Whitleys, an aircraft long past its prime, whereas other OTUs were converting to the Vickers Wellington. Nos 24 and 81 OTU, based at Whitchurch, were to carry on flying the aged Whitley until at least the middle of 1944.

1943 brought very little change to Honeybourne and Long Marston. Two days into the new year Whitley EB389 was lost with all its crew when taking off for a high-level bombing sortie. At 23.39 hrs it exploded in mid-air and crashed near Shipston-on-Stour in Warwickshire, the cause of the explosion being the premature firing of a photoflash. These were used to record bombs or leaflets dropped on targets during night operations and should have been placed in the flare chute, to fire in conjunction with the bomb release circuitry. The catastrophe was caused because a photoflash was already in the tube. The crew would not have had time to realise what was happening.

The Avro Anson – taxi for most Ferry pilots. (MAP)

An upgrading of Honeybourne took place at the end of January when Mark II Drem airfield lighting was installed along the perimeter track and various other areas. This was to support the quicker and safer movement of aircraft on the ground. January weather hampered the training programme but five further 'nickelling' operations were flown during the month. Several aircraft became disoriented due to the weather but the 'Darky' system then in operation saved the situation in each case.

'Darky' had been introduced fully in 1942, when a small transmitter/receiver (T/R) with a limited range was installed in every operational and non-operational aircraft including those of the OTUs. The 'Darky' ground station was also equipped with a T/R, usually manned by WAAFs. The principle was that the aircraft in distress would transmit on the 'Darky' frequency whilst circling the area in which it was lost, several times. The transmission would be picked up by the ground receiving station and would alert local searchlight batteries. They in turn would switch on three beams to culminate in a cone to direct the aircraft to the nearest landing ground. Although it did not work in every case, many aircrew had reason to be grateful to the system.

One trainee pilot of 24 OTU who wished to remain anonymous related how 'Darky' saved him and his crew: 'We were part of a force of six Whitleys that left Long Marston at around 19.00 hrs to drop leaflets near Paris. We left in pretty bad weather that gradually got worse over France. As we completed the operation and turned for home, the cloud base was down to about 800 ft. We crossed what we thought was the French or Dutch coast but could have been anywhere. We continued on the bearing given which should have enabled us to cross the UK coast at around the Dover area. Working on the ETA principle, I let down when we were time-expired, hoping to see the coastline. Still the thick cloud persisted, to around 500 ft now, plus it was getting fairly dark. I asked the wireless operator to switch on "Darky" which he did. By now we were very low on fuel and I braced myself to tell the crew to get ready to bale out. Suddenly a piercing light lit up the underside of the cloud. Then another and another. Slowly moving together they formed a single cone which began to move to our port side. Following the cone we saw a glimmer of straight lights ahead. A runway! Firing off a flare and flashing our identification, we came down lower and overflew the airfield before "turning finals" (i.e. making the final turn and coming in to land). As we touched down the searchlights went out to be followed by the flarepath lights lest an enemy aircraft was about. Pulling the old Whitley to a stop, the engines gulped the last drop of fuel. We had landed at Wellesbourne Mountford and the ground could not have been sweeter. Without "Darky" we might all have perished and lost another aircraft.'

A return made to 91 Group in March 1943 showed the unit's strength at 55 Whitleys, 11 Ansons, a Defiant and 2 Lysanders. Both local and command 'Bullseyes' were an increasing part of the training programme together with further 'nickelling'. For the pupil aircrew nearing the finish of their courses, it was time to see at first hand the type of four-engined bomber they would be flying on operations. The usual demonstration aircraft was a Halifax but on occasions, the reward would be a Lancaster.

The 'Wings for Victory' campaign had gathered pace over the past year. After the popular slogan exhorting everyone to give their 'Pots and Pans to Make a Spitfire', 'Wings for Victory' had captured the public's interest. Nearly every town or city in the UK wanted to take part and those around Honeybourne and Long Marston were no exception. With most of the local towns coming together at Evesham, three Whitleys flew over in formation as the Station Commander took the salute near the town hall.

One of the indispensable reporting organisations at this time was the Observer Corps, who operated from positions known simply as 'posts'. Their peak of operation was during the Battle of Britain when several of the Chain Home radar stations were put out of action by the enemy. They then became the ears and eyes of Fighter Command. Broadway Tower near Evesham in Worcestershire was such a post. It was manned by Observers Albert Lowe and Ernest Hollington, whose main duty was to report enemy aircraft within the area together with any unusual incidents. At 14.15 hrs on 2 June 1943 they heard the sound of aero engines. It was a cloudy day and therefore they could not see the aircraft. With hills surrounding the entire area they knew that to fly low could be dangerous indeed. As the sound got closer they realised that it was an aircraft in distress. Straining their eyes in the hope of seeing whether it was friend or enemy, the sound of engines was replaced by a tremendous explosion. Both men ran towards where the sound had come from to be confronted by an appalling scene. A ball of fire was rising to the sky with parts of the aircraft scattered around. Running towards the main fuselage, which was still intact, and with no thought for their own safety, they managed to pull five of the crew away from the inferno. It was too late to save four of them, but the fifth crewman, Sgt G.E. Ekins, was found to be alive albeit with horrific injuries and burns. Sadly, although help was summoned directly the crash happened, Sgt Ekins died shortly after. This terrible tragedy shocked both stations. Both Observers were later mentioned in the *London Gazette* and also received a certificate signed by Winston Churchill praising their brave efforts on that day.

A very subdued Honeybourne and Long Marston got back to the usual programme of training and flying 'nickels'. Six were flown in June and seven in July, all of them giving valuable experience for the crews when moving on to operational squadrons. The latter month saw Anson DJ242 TY-U involved in an emergency landing. Taking off from Honeybourne at 22.17 hrs for a night exercise, PO K. Smith with a crew of six was nearing the end of a successful sortie and thinking of returning to base when the starboard engine cut out. Realising that he would not make the airfield, he managed to crash-land the aircraft on the main road leading to Evesham. All crew members survived with minor injuries to PO Smith.

With 1943 seeing the demand for aircrew even greater, the station strength during August had risen to 1,727 with 814 resident at Long Marston. The 'Battle of the Ruhr' meant that although sporadic raids were being carried out on Berlin, it was the centres of war production that were priority targets for Bomber Command. Italy was also a target for many squadrons. All of this however required no participation from Honeybourne with the exception of further pressure being put upon the OTU to train aircrew that much quicker.

The autumn of 1943 saw it still struggling on with the now very ageing Whitleys. Although they were mainly the Mark V, several were going unserviceable on the ground whilst others had to return early from sorties with mechanical problems. Two tragic accidents in October again shocked both stations. Whitley EB347 left Long Marston at 20.35 hrs for high level bombing practice. At 21.30 hrs it crashed at Old Manor Farm in Warwickshire and burnt out with the loss of the entire crew. Three days later Whitley V EB348, again taking off from Long Marston, crashed near Waterbeach airfield in Cambridgeshire with the loss of the crew, the first all-Canadian crew to be lost in the OTU. In October, twelve leaflet dropping sorties were carried out, and ten in November. The following month saw 78 'nickels' carried out by 91 Group, 21 of them being flown by 24 OTU, a considerable effort.

Bomber Command now entered the period known as 'the Battle for Berlin'. The all-out assault on the city began on the nights of 18/19 November 1943 and would continue relentlessly for the next four and a half months. Between 19 November and the end of January 1944, 7,403 sorties were flown against the city incurring the loss of 384 aircraft and countless crews. There is no doubt that the raids caused severe damage in Berlin but the heavy losses did have an effect on the morale of the bomber crews. This undoubtedly also had an effect on the trainees and instructors of the OTUs. Despite this, Christmas was celebrated with an air of expectancy that this could be the last year of the war. As if to prove this theory wrong, an air raid warning was sounded on 3 January 1944 at 00.05 hrs. An enemy aircraft was heard within the area as all sections of Honeybourne went to action stations and the station status became red. (This appears to be the only time this action was implemented.) After 15 minutes the 'all clear' sounded and the status went back to black.

'Nickelling' operations were carried out throughout January 1944, several ending in mishaps. February was to prove a disappointing month when three Whitleys were involved in accidents. Whitley V N1375 collided with Z6673 on the runway. Confusion between the airfield control officer and two airmen stationed at the upwind end of the runway regarding lighting messages was found to be the cause. In Z6673 Flt Lt Mathews, DFC, was under the impression that he had been cleared to backtrack. Sadly he lost his life in the collision. The same day, 12 February, Whitley V BD238 encountered severe icing, which led to the loss of the starboard engine. Wisely the crew took to their parachutes, leaving the aircraft to crash at Ledbury in Herefordshire.

In order to assist training, a number of Miles Martinet aircraft were attached to the OTU. Designed from the outset as a target tug, the Martinet had made its maiden flight on 24 April 1942. Full scale production began months later whereupon a total of 1,724 were built, production finally ending in 1945. It was fitted with either a wind-driven or motorised winch that carried six flag and sleeve drogue targets. Martinets gradually replaced Lysanders and Battles in the target role until they themselves were replaced by Hurricanes in June 1944.

1st March saw authorisation given to the OTUs to carry bombs whilst on 'nickelling' operations. Half the Whitley force would carry 4 x 500lb HE bombs whilst the other half would carry small bomb containers. For Bomber Command, Berlin was still the main target with the RAF bombing the city by night and the USAAF bombing by day. Over 2,500 tons of bombs were dropped on Berlin in one raid during March.

After seeing the OTU through a very difficult period. Gp Cpt A.C.P. Carver relinquished his command to Gp Cpt G.V. Lane, DFC, AFC, on 28 March 1944. Three weeks later news arrived that 91 Group had sanctioned 24 OTU to convert from Whitleys to Wellingtons. Over the next few months a rapid conversion course would take place with a total of 54 Wellington Xs replacing the Whitleys. Many said 'better late than never' but at this stage of the war, the four-engined heavy bombers such as the Halifax and the Lancaster were the backbone of Bomber Command, releasing more twin-engined bombers to a training role. The last of the bomber variants, the Wellington X, remained in service until 1953, proving the strength and versatility of the geodetic method of construction designed by Barnes Wallis. For some time the change-over incurred flying both the Whitley and the Wellington but as crews converted to the latter, the Whitleys were taken to other OTUs and maintenance units.

The Wellington was newer than the Whitley, although not by much, and the trainee aircrews and groundcrews were glad to receive the type. With no break in the training routine, the 'nickelling' and bombing of enemy targets continued. For some months there had been rumours circulating that a second front was soon to be established on the Continent. On 5 June 1944 a signal was received at both stations ordering all aircraft to be grounded for a period of at least 48 hours. The reason soon became obvious when in the early hours of the 6th, the sound of aero engines filled the air above Honeybourne and

Wellingtons of 149 Squadron with Honeybourne-trained crews aboard. (A. Thomas)

Long Marston as Dakotas, many towing gliders, thundered their way to the French coast. Operation 'Overlord', the D-Day invasion had begun. For several days Honeybourne and Long Marston accepted many diverted aircraft returning from the Continent – Dakotas, Halifaxes, Lancasters, all of them very glad to land at any airfield. With so many aircraft in the sky at one time, some did not make it home, unfortunately coming down in the cold Channel. As part of their training routine, crews and aircraft from 24 OTU took part in Air Sea Rescue searches. Their duty was to spot any dinghies in the water and report the position to enable a rescue launch to be deployed.

As with the Whitleys, there were to be tragic accidents with the Wellingtons, many incurring severe loss of life. One such occurred on 14th July when Wellington HE381 (TY-G) crashed near Long Compton in Warwickshire. Taking off from Honeybourne at 11.53 hrs for a circuit and landing exercise, two minutes into the flight the aircraft got into a spin and fell from the sky. FO J.A. Thompson (pilot RCAF), WO R. Burns (w/op RCAF), Sgt J.C. Anderson (AG RCAF) and Flt Sgt J.W. Johnston (AG RCAF) were killed outright. The three Canadians were taken to Brookwood Military Cemetery whilst WO Burns was buried in his native Scotland. It is believed that he was the last RAF airman (not of commissioned rank) to be killed serving with 24 OTU.

Wellington TY-V of 'B' Flight, No 24 OTU. (A. Thomas)

The last Whitley to fly with the unit left Honeybourne in July, most glad to see it go. Though the type had served the unit well, due to their age maintenance on them had become an ever more desperate struggle. The Whitley had been one of the mainstays of Bomber Command in the early years of the war and would be remembered mainly for its pioneering work on leaflet dropping. Its relegation to training duties in 1942 gave it a new lease of life but it was never a favourite with the trainee aircrews or the groundcrews.

August saw a double tragedy when two Wellingtons collided over the bombing range at Longdon. It happened around 23.00 hrs when MF591 struck the port wing of LP618 causing severe damage. As the latter spun out of control, just one member of the crew, Flt Lt Bruce, managed to bale out. The rest, FS H.G. Round, Sgt L.H. Frazer, Sgt L.M. Lysak, Sgt L.C. Lamb, Sgt G.O. Prime and Sgt A.E. Kidney, all Canadians, perished in the crash. Meanwhile MF591, with its nose torn away, was skilfully flown by FO W.W. McSween (RCAF) to crash-land at RAF Defford. Sadly, the impact of the mid-air crash had thrown PO Shwaikoski (RCAF) out of the bomb aimer's position, causing him to fall to his death. September was to prove another bad month when three Wellingtons crashed with the loss of six aircrew.

Remaining Maycrete huts at Honeybourne. (Author)

This last full year of the war saw the accident rate for the OTUs drop sharply. Only 13 aircraft were damaged beyond repair in December 1944 compared with 29 major accidents for the same month a year earlier. Now that the Allies were closing on Berlin, the number of 'nickelling' operations dropped dramatically and this in turn helped the casualty rate.

Demand for new crews, however, did not seem to be diminishing. Nineteen OTUs, including No 24, would continue to perform this role for the Command. Between 1 and 24 April 1945, the unit flew more than 3,139 hours. The European war ended from 00.01 hrs on 9 May 1945.

The previous day had seen the two stations celebrate the final victory. Gp Cpt Lane addressed all personnel telling them what a superb job the OTU had done but reminding them that the war in Japan was far from over. Formalities over, a party began which was to last until the early hours of the morning. With no official notification to stand down, flying training continued for the next few days. As if in a swansong, 11 May 1945 saw the final incident before disbandment. A Wellington X left Honeybourne on a night navigating exercise. Whilst

Honeybourne watch office (control tower), now converted to a private house. (Author)

flying over East Anglia the starboard engine failed and the pilot, FO M.A. East (RCAF), attempted to land at Langham airfield. In doing so he overshot the runway and crashed in a neighbouring village. Although three cottages and a YMCA building were hit, no loss of civilian life was incurred. Sadly, FO G.J. Hay (RCAF) was killed when his rear turret broke away from the fuselage, and the remaining five crew members were all injured. This was the last serious accident to befall 24 OTU, which finally disbanded on 24th July.

The satellite at Long Marston was the first to go to Care and Maintenance when the Wellingtons based there returned to Honeybourne. From that time on, disbandment came fast. On 11th August, No 21 OTU moved into the station from Enstone while their own runways were under repair. VJ Day was celebrated on 15th August, heralding the end of the global conflict. 21 OTU returned to Enstone and in October, silence descended upon Honeybourne.

By November 1945, 91 Group had handed both airfields over to 41 Group, Maintenance Command for the storage of surplus aircraft. This was to continue until July 1948 when the stations were once again placed under Care and Maintenance. Some of the land was returned to its previous owners whilst buildings were offered to Evesham Rural District Council for development. This is the condition in which we find Honeybourne today. Many buildings remain – hangars, Nissen and Maycrete huts, shelters etc – most used by local industry. The runways have been broken up and returned to agriculture whilst the control tower is now a private house.

The OTUs deserve recognition for their contribution to Bomber Command. Without the commitment of these units in delivering new aircrew to the main force, the war might have gone on much longer. No 24 OTU, Honeybourne and its satellite airfield were part of that commitment.

6
MADLEY

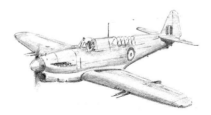

Situated six miles west-southwest of Hereford, Madley was not initially considered for an airfield due to the close proximity of hills all around. It was reconsidered for construction, however, by the spring of 1940 and became a busy training station for the duration of the war. One of its most famous trainees was the comedian and writer, Eric Sykes, who remembered it well, and in 1945 it played a part in one of the strangest stories of the Second World War, that of Rudolf Hess.

Being an agricultural area, much of the land under consideration in 1940 was farmed, in particular land belonging to Street House Farm at Madley. In a letter dated 4 October 1940, the Under Secretary of State at the Air Ministry notified the farm's owner, Donald Parsons, of the immediate and compulsory requisition of 27 acres of arable land. The expansion also included land belonging to Hartley's, the jam manufacturers. The factory and strawberry plantation were engulfed within the dispersed site, which covered land as far as Webton village. This site included the instructional area, sick quarters, three wing mess sites and officers' and airmen's quarters.

The main airfield site, which now included land from Street House, Broad Green, Parkway and Little Brampton farms, had a typical bomber airfield layout consisting of three grass runways, three pre-war Hinaidi hangars, two Callender-Hamilton hangars, together with 13 Blister hangars and the usual selection of flight offices, maintenance blocks, gas decontamination centre and station headquarters alongside the hangars.

By 1941 the airfield was still in various stages of construction. The main contractors, Mowlem, brought in 36 busloads of workers every day. Working from 7 am until 6 pm seven days a week, the weather was the only problem to hamper progress. One essential not laid at this

Sergeant Peter Jones (kneeling left) with fellow trainees at Madley, 1944, showing the heavy flying suits and boots worn to keep warm. (Peter Jones)

time was a running water system. However, basic facilities were put in place consisting of large water containers and Elsan latrines together with Nissen huts with a central coal-burning stove for the airmen's accommodation. Being two separate sites and divided into 21 separate areas, personnel had to walk from the airfield to the dispersed site, a distance of about half a mile, every mealtime and whenever they wanted a wash in the communal washhouse. After doing this once or twice there was a rapid increase in the number of bicycles being used by airmen and airwomen. The intersection between the main airfield and the domestic site was frequently referred to as 'Piccadilly Circus'.

For an airman, life was just that little bit unbearable. One such person was Peter Jones: 'I was stationed at No 4 Radio School, RAF Madley, late 1943 to 1944. It was a good posting for me as I originated from Hereford. The camp covered a large area, so much so that a local saying was "Never have so many walked so far for so little"! We walked nearly all day from our billets to the school classrooms and the airfield. We used to carry all our belongings with us in a side-pack but this was eventually stopped by the chief medical officer because we were getting lop-sided shoulders. Orders then came through that we had to carry our rucksacks on our backs so that our shoulders were balanced. What we carried was nobody's business: our eating utensils, radio gear, classroom books, PT gear, flying boots and sometimes a rifle.

'We used to live in tin huts; they were very cold in the winter due to lack of fuel and so hot in the summer. We had five blankets altogether. Aircrew were privileged to have two white sheets, in fact it was not very nice to sleep between the blankets because they were so rough. If by any chance we could not obtain sheets straight away, we had to use newspaper at the top of the bed where the blankets turned over otherwise you would have a red neck in the morning. So, on top of the bed we had four double blankets plus an overcoat to keep us warm during the winter months.

'To have our meals we had to walk about two miles there and back which was not too bad when you consider that other places around the camp were four miles there and back.'

Another problem was the lack of electricity as no main supply was available at that time. A generator, some say identical to that installed in the liner *Queen Mary*, was found to supply the entire camp with light. However, the one good point was that the domestic site was on the edge of Kingstone village, which did at least have a shop and a decent pub!

When it was officially opened on 27 August 1941, the advance party of officers and airmen found Madley far from completion. This meant they had to live at RAF Hereford and travel in each day until the dispersed site became habitable. When it did so, it fell to No 4 Signals School to inaugurate Madley, with the first trainees arriving on 28 November 1941. The duty of the school was to train 2,800 ground and 1,200 aircrew wireless operators (Wop). This training was usually combined with that of an air gunner (AG) as the aircrew trade at that time was that of Wop/AG, the latter requiring a four-week course at an Air Gunnery School. This was in addition to the number of Wop/AGs already being trained at OTUs such as Pershore. For the wireless operator training, a number of Percival Proctors and de Havilland Dominie aircraft arrived.

The single-engined Proctor was a military version of the Vega Gull light sport and touring aircraft. It was the Proctor IV that came to Madley, this being the radio trainer version which could accommodate four people. Like the Fairey Battles at Pershore, the Proctor IV was built by a subcontractor, in this case F. Hills and Sons of Manchester. Powered by a single 210 hp de Havilland Gipsy Queen II engine, it had a cruising speed of 140 mph at 3,000 ft and a range of 500 miles. In contrast the twin-engined de Havilland Dominie was a military

An ex-RAF Percival Proctor, now in civilian livery. (MAP)

A de Havilland Dragon Rapide, the civilian version of the Dominie used to train wireless operators at Madley. (Author)

version of then-famous Dragon Rapide light airliner, powered by two 200 hp de Havilland Gipsy VI engines. Once again, some building of the Dominie was subcontracted to Brush Coachworks. It was a five- or six-seat radio trainer fitted with a Direction Finding Loop and had a maximum speed of 157 mph at 1,000 ft. The final number of aircraft allocated to No 4 Signals School was 60 Proctor IVs and 18 Dominies.

Mrs J.M. Elkington, the wife of one pilot who flew the Proctor for the trainees recalls what he told her of his life at Madley: 'My late husband was a Sgt pilot in the RAFVR from 1941 until 1946 and at one time was stationed at RAF Madley. Although in a reserved occupation he was allowed to enlist for flying duties. After his flying training, part of which was done at Cranwell, a fact that he was very proud of, he was sent to do, as he put it, a "stooge" job at Madley flying wing. It was No 4 Signals School where obviously radio operators were trained. All the pilots had to do was take the trainees up and about. I remember he said there were quite a few planes flown by "hot-heads" which sometimes crashed on the Brecon Beacons and Black Mountains. He would often speak of those days.'

A painting of a signals training Dominie showing the Direction Finding Loop. (Les Vowles)

Another person with fond memories of Madley was Sgt Basil Shillaker: 'The sole purpose of the base was the training of wireless operators. Due to the distance involved between the two sites, we carried our side packs at all times which contained washing and eating implements and notebooks etc. The training period lasted about six months, based on a six-day week of eight hours a day, excluding lunch times, guard duties and Sunday church parades. The guard duties consisted of looking after aircraft on the far side of the airfield in shifts of two hours on and four hours off. Once we started flying we had an increase of two shillings a day. This to us was a big increase as up to that time we were only being paid three shillings. At the same time we were issued with full flying kit which filled a second kitbag and made it hard going if you were posted and at some point had to carry your own kit.

'The aircraft in use at that time were the de Havilland Dominie and the Percival Proctor. The Dominie was for initial instruction and had an instructor with five trainees. Its wireless equipment was the

Ken Summerlin, sporting his Signallers brevet, trained at Madley. (K. Summerlin)

A training school session at Madley. Note the W/Op flash on the sleeve of the sergeant on the left hand side. (Crown)

Marconi Transmitter T1154 with the Receiver T1155. These were for use with Morse Code as it was the only way to communicate over the necessary distances. Aircraft were fitted with radio telegraphy and Direction Finding apparatus but it had only a short range and was mainly used by pilots. The Proctor was used for final flying wireless telegraphy tests which consisted of five one-hour flights working the ground stations.

'Whether by luck or judgement, I managed to achieve over seventy per cent in all the tests. At one of these I was flying with a new chief instructor, a Wing Commander. He had already given some of us a pep talk and luckily all went well. I understand the ground staff were in a great flap over the fact he had insisted on observing a flying test. I have particular memories of this flight as the Proctor had a poor safety record and we were advised how to bale out depending which spin the aircraft went into. In fact, I did witness a Proctor tumbling down and at the same time a parachute opening. It had collided with another Proctor on the landing approach. I learnt later that the pilot also

Trainees practising sending Morse code at Madley. (Imperial War Museum)

parachuted down and sustained a broken leg. These were apparently the few occasions when anyone had baled out of a Proctor successfully. When I returned to my hut later in the day the engine from one of the aircraft was laying a few feet away.

'Although the Proctor had a bad record the Dominie was comparatively good and to my knowledge the school only had one bad crash over the Black Mountains. Sadly, all on board were killed. During the war I witnessed a number of fatal crashes and in one instance saw a dead pilot. However, in my mind was always the thought that it can't happen to me. That is not to say I wasn't scared at times.'

Much of the time spent on instruction was taken up by classes. The primary subject was the Morse Code in which airmen had to receive speeds of 18, 20 and 22 words per minute in both plain language and Bomber code (which was four letters per unit). It was the Morse Code speed that most trainees failed on. It was this lack of aptitude in Morse sending and receiving that was probably the biggest single reason for failure on wireless operator courses down through the years. So much so that it was decided to start Morse training at an early stage, at the Recruit Training Centre, Blackpool.

One person to become totally proficient at Morse and pass out with flying colours was Eric Sykes. With his permission I quote from his autobiography, *If I Don't Write It, Nobody Else Will*:

LAC Eric Sykes, radio operator at Madley, 1943. (Eric Sykes via Norma Farnes)

'The most important part of our training at Blackpool was learning the Morse Code, essential to wireless operators. Our schoolrooms were at the Winter Gardens, a venue I played many times years afterwards in a more peaceful, pleasurable age. Incidentally, the mastering of the Morse Code was a doddle for me, I was already proficient and could send and receive in Morse Code as fast, and in some cases faster, than some of the instructors. I'd mastered this skill when I was sixteen in order to be a wireless operator in the Merchant Navy. And so here I was in an extraordinary, sunny Blackpool, marching, drilling, doing rifle practice and dozing through the lazy afternoons in the Winter Gardens. The weeks rushed by too quickly for my liking. I was now conversing with my instructors at a speed too fast for ordinary erks. I was suntanned to a deep walnut, clear eyed and bushy tailed. I even looked forward to guard duty, although we were only guarding Marks and Spencer's. It was heady stuff! After sixteen weeks of high summer in Blackpool, I thought the war was a doddle and felt privileged to have been invited to take part. The passing out parade on the forecourt of the Metropole Hotel filled me with exultation, I even considered signing on for a full twelve years, it wasn't such a bad career. But I didn't quite know it all, I still had a lot to learn and eagerly scanning the noticeboard every morning for the where-abouts of my posting, I didn't care where it was. Any operational airfield would suffice. At least I would be sending and receiving messages that mattered, chatting up members of the WAAF with aeroplanes taking off one after another for Berlin or the Ruhr. My heart leapt when I saw my name on the noticeboard the following day. I had been posted to a place in Herefordshire called Madley. As I stood before the corporal in the guardroom who was making out my movement order I asked if Madley was a fighter or a bomber station. Without looking up he said, "If you see a fighter or a bomber at Madley, he's lost." I didn't get it and as he handed me my documents he took pity on me. "All in good time, laddie. You're still in training and if I were you I wouldn't be in such a hurry to put my head on the block." I didn't get that either. What it is to be ignorant!

'Madley itself may be a delightful little town but the place where the three-ton lorries deposited us in the early darkness preceding the onset of winter, was barren and pockmarked by Nissen huts, corrugated iron and concrete floors – Blackpool had hardly prepared us for this. The first morning dawned cold and grey. It seemed like only yesterday we were in shirtsleeves, basking in the golden summer of Blackpool. Greatcoats were now the order of the day. We were paraded and after a short address, the CO gave us a lot more information, which was mainly carried away on the brisk east wind. He then called four of us out and we became class leaders. Our duties were not too onerous, we had to line up our allotted section and then march them off to the classes. Afterwards we marched them back again and when we shouted "Halt" and "Dismiss" our responsibility was at an end. We were in Madley for further training on the complex inside of a wireless set and naturally a quicker, more competent way of receiving and sending messages in Morse Code, call signs, contact, wavelengths – in fact everything a wireless operator should know. I was beginning to wonder when, and if ever, we would be posted on real active service. The only aircraft we'd seen up to now were Halifaxes, Blenheims, Messerschmitts, Dorniers and Spitfires, but unfortunately they were all hanging from the ceiling of one of the classrooms! When would we be posted to an aerodrome? I fervently hoped to fly as a wireless operator air gunner.

'At last one grey, blustery morning the noticeboard was full with postings. Eager faces scanned the board and there was an electricity in the wind. I found myself alone, searching the noticeboard for my name. It wasn't there. Full of old madam, I strode in to the administration offices and demanded to see the CO. The corporal I addressed was startled out of his wits. This was quite out of order: no erk had ever marched in before and demanded to see the Lord God Almighty. Then came the understanding. "Are you 1522813 Sykes?" he said. I said "Yes" and the mystery was solved. He handed me a travel warrant for me to go home for seven days' leave. When I asked why I hadn't gone with the others, he told me that they'd all passed out with the rank of AC2 whereas I had been promoted to AC1. Wonderful! He further told me that I was posted to Swaffham in Norfolk. Telling this to a sergeant later he told me there was no airfield at Swaffham. Mystified, I went on leave and after seven days reported to the said place at Swaffham. It was not an airfield but an army base, part of the Second Army being assembled for an assault on the coast of Europe. Here I was awarded the coveted Wop/Ag badge consisting of a clenched fist clutching bolts of lightning. Although hopeful of flying, I never did make it into the air but I certainly saw war.'

As D-Day approached, Eric was part of a mobile signals unit, No 589A MSU, attached to the army. He eventually became one of the first men from his unit to land on French soil several days after D-Day.

Meanwhile, back at Madley training continued in radio theory, visual Morse, wireless equipment, aircraft layout of facilities, aircraft

The radio sets that Madley-trained wireless operators used. (Author)

recognition, use of the parachute and a limited amount of navigation theory. Day after day the trainees would struggle with sending and receiving Morse, many of them not attaining the desired level and forced to re-muster to another trade.

Peter Jones takes up the story once again: 'Radio training at Madley was very hard, you did not have much time for yourself. Up at 6 am, shave in the dark because there were no light bulbs in the ablutions, they used to take the bulbs for the huts! Walk one mile for breakfast and then on to the classrooms etc until about 6 pm. You then had other duties as well as homework and "genning up" for the next day. The instructors were very good, most of them were ex-teachers and taught us very well. Flying was fun, especially around Herefordshire and the Black Mountains, although you did not have much time to look out and around. At one time we had two wireless operators on the Proctor plus the pilot and all the radio equipment etc. Halfway through the flight we had to change over operators and sometimes this changeover became dangerous for the pilot. So much so that some nearly lost control of the aircraft. Consequently this was stopped and only one operator was allowed on the Proctors. The Dominies were used for special duties and carried six or seven operators. Special duties included such procedures as getting fixed positions and bearings from the air in case you got lost in any way. The Free French Air Force came to Madley for training at the same time as I was there. I remember when we were marching we were saying "left-right" etc and they were saying "un-deux"!

'Although it is now 58 years since I was there, certain occasions stick in your mind. One of them concerns the trailing aerial we used on the aircraft. The pilot would usually inform the wireless operator when he was about to land but this did not always happen so on many times the trailing aerial with lead weights on the end was not reeled back in before landing. Once, when the pilot forgot to tell the operator, the aerial got wrapped around some telephone wires and brought them down, causing much correspondence between the RAF and GPO. If you lost the aerial on landing this could cost the wireless operator the sum of 15 shillings. I am glad to say I never had to pay, guess I was lucky. The unfortunate ones that did have to pay were not dropped from the trade but others who did not come up to the required level of expertise were re-mustered to other trades.' Peter Jones was to spend eleven months at Madley.

In July 1941 another unit became resident at Madley. No 8 Anti-Aircraft Co-operation Unit operated a few Westland Lysanders to help local anti-aircraft gunners practise their range prediction and firing techniques. They had moved from Pembridge Landing Ground, just a short distance away, whilst it was upgraded to airfield status. That eventually became RAF Shobdon with the Lysanders being equally shared between both airfields.

Being close to the Welsh mountains, it was decided to base a Mountain Rescue Team at Madley. Previous aircraft incidents had been dealt with by medical staff from the sick quarters at either Madley or Shobdon. This practice obviously interfered with the training programme and with an increase in accidents due to poor weather conditions, a fully trained team had been formed by 1943.

As the radio school increased in size over the coming months there were certain benefits to the local community. Being a training airfield, a lot of trainees were allowed home at weekends and of course they took their annual holidays. The catering section at Madley were somehow not aware of this fact as Joyce Cottam, the daughter of landowner Donald Parsons recalls: 'My dad kept pigs on the farm and he came to an arrangement with the cookhouse on the airfield to collect the waste food to turn into pig swill. When the weekends or holidays came, the same amount of food was cooked but of course, the waste increased. They still baked around 80 loaves of bread and cakes and on these occasions, dad used to bring home what was thrown out for us all to eat. Lovely fresh baked bread and cakes, things that in wartime you could only dream of. On these occasions the pigs went without the usual amount of swill as it was distributed to the local neighbours. To think we were all on rations yet the cookhouse was throwing food away.'

Day after day the school would carry out its training programme and the local area would be filled with the sound of aero engines. The weather during the winter months was responsible for many crashes and it was the duty of the daily diarist to record them in the Madley Operations Record Book. They usually did so in a very 'matter of fact' manner:

'January 7th 1942 – Weather adverse to flying conditions – Heavy snow making visibility poor. Difficulty was experienced by pilots when landing some of the Proctor aircraft. Two minor crashes took place without injury or serious consequences.'

'October 3rd 1942 – Proctor DX218 – accident due to burst tyre. Damage to undercarriage, propeller and wing. No casualties. In the afternoon another accident – Proctor DZ181 crash-landed due to wet weather. Minor injuries suffered by crew.'

It was not, however, all doom and gloom. The diarist happily recorded the arrival of the WAAFs on 3 March 1942, together with the fact that many of the pilots and aircrew attending the courses were Czech and Polish.

Many of the local people came to recognise the sound of a particular engine but occasionally a different type would be heard. On 8 May 1942 several Curtiss Tomahawks of No 26 Squadron were detached to Madley from Gatwick. Although designated a low level tactical reconnaissance aircraft, the Tomahawks were to be used in the anti-aircraft co-operation role. A similar role was carried out by two Hurricanes and two Mustangs of No 239 Squadron which also detached to Madley from Gatwick for a short period during an army co-operation exercise.

It had been noticed for some time, that with the arrival of heavier aircraft, whenever it rained the grass runways at Madley became muddy and very rutted. It was decided to lay Sommerfeld Track and in October 1943, an RAF Construction Unit arrived to commence work. These units had originally consisted of military and civilian personnel but by 1943 had expanded to 20 squadrons employing military personnel only. With the enemy raids on airfields mainly over by 1942, the construction squadrons were put to work on lengthening or strengthening runways. The Sommerfeld Track was eventually removed and Madley got three tarmac and concrete runways.

Training continued at an increased pace due to the demands of operational flying. Bomber Command, although achieving better results under the leadership of Arthur Harris, were suffering enormous losses during late 1943 and early 1944. Every time a bomber was lost, seven or eight crew members were lost with it. The nightly raids carried out by the Command placed a huge burden on the training units to supply even more aircrew trained in the various trades. As the efficiency and technicalities of the radio apparatus improved, so the training became longer and more specialised.

Sgt Basil Shillaker again recalls: 'There was at this time a small contingent of French naval trainees doing the same course as ourselves. The majority of them were fishermen who had escaped from occupied France. Their pilots were all French officers and to us their uniforms seemed very ornate as compared with the RAF. Unfortunately, from what I remember their safety record was not

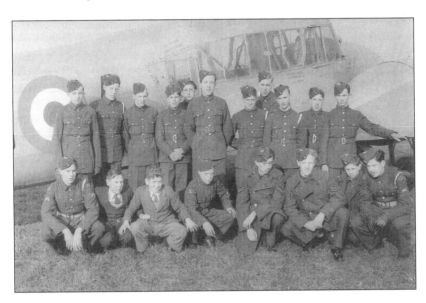

A group of Air Cadets helping out at Madley circa 1944. (Maureen Beauchamp via D. Foxton)

The crew of the B-24G Liberator Bold Venture III *that flew unaided and crashed at Hereford. (Bob Collis)*

good. Proportionally their losses of Proctors were far greater than the base as a whole. I finally completed my training about the middle of 1944 and at a small ceremony received my S brevet and was promoted to Sergeant.'

As Sgt Shillaker celebrated his promotion over that Christmas period, one of the more unusual incidents in the history of Madley occurred. Whilst the King was making his traditional Christmas Day speech on 25 December, an American Consolidated B-24 Liberator of the 467th Bombardment Group named *Bold Venture III* was struggling to cross enemy territory after a bombing raid. Being Christmas, it was known as a 'milk run', meaning that as the enemy would also be celebrating the festive season they would not be at their most alert. For the pilot, Paul Ehrlich, it was his 25th mission and he was therefore due to return home. He volunteered for the Christmas Day operation not knowing that it would end so dramatically. It seems as though the ground flak units in occupied Europe were certainly alert as the Liberator came under attack. Flying over Belgium a shell exploded behind the seat of the pilot, fragments of which embedded themselves in his left leg. Flying at 23,000 ft, the crew were on oxygen when another piece of flak tore off Captain Ehrlich's oxygen mask, badly damaging his chin. With flames now appearing around one of the engines and without oxygen he became disoriented and realised that he could no longer fly the aircraft.

Hitting the alarm bell to warn the rest of the crew that they were to bale out, and setting the aircraft on autopilot, Captain Ehrlich and the flight deck crew took to their parachutes and leapt out of the aircraft to land in Germany and become POWs. The remaining six crew, having heard the alarm bell, took off their flak suits and attached their parachutes. Realising that the aircraft was still flying straight they hesitated and waited for the alarm bell to go again. When it did not ring the bombardier, John Beyer, attempted to call the captain on the intercom. He did not realise that his intercom cord had become disconnected and therefore received no answer from the flight deck. Making their way forward, the crew looked for the legs of the pilot which could be normally seen through a small hatch. Seeing none, they realised that they were on their own in the aircraft and prepared to exit rather swiftly. By now the aircraft was over Allied France and after jumping and landing successfully, the six crewmen were taken into Allied hands to fight another day.

Meanwhile the aircraft, rapidly running out of fuel, carried on its set course to cross the English coastline and continue inland. By now all the dials in the cockpit were past the danger mark and, slowly losing height, the last remnants of fuel were used up. Crossing Herefordshire, the Liberator narrowly missed a group of houses before ploughing into the ground at St Margarets near Vowchurch.

As *Bold Venture III* was coming down to earth, the rescue services at Madley prepared for what they thought would be a grisly operation. When they reached the aircraft, which had remained virtually intact, they were amazed to find no signs of any crew. What they did find was the bodies of three cows that were in the field and had got in the way of the stricken aircraft. Being wartime, no reporting of the incident was made except to the military authorities. It was not until the end of the war that the whole incredible story was told.

With the war now going the Allies' way, three days before D-Day Madley received a signal that General George S. Patton Junior was to make a scheduled stop at the airfield. A hastily convened guard of honour greeted him on his arrival and although he could not divulge when the landings were to take place, his presence indicated that it would not be long.

No 4 RADIO SCHOOL - MAT

Date	Hour	Aircraft Type and No. DOMINIE	Pilot	Du
8.6.43	13.35	X 7500	F/o Payne	
8.6.43	15.45	X 7500	F/o Payne	
8.6.43	18.00	X 7447	F/o Munell	
6.6.43	13.35	X 7440	F/s Drew	
6.6.43	15.25	X 7440	F/S Drew	
11.6.43	14.00	X 7501	F/o Munell	
11.6.43	15.50	X 7501	F/o Munell	
14.6.43	08.35	X 7441	F/s Mackintosh	
14.6.43	10.35	X 7441	F/S Mackintosh	
17.6.43	08.35	X 7485	F/S Clarke	
17.6.43	10.30	X 7485 PROCTOR	F/S Clarke	
22.6.43	11.35	Z 7259	Sgt. Howarth	
22.6.43	15.00	HM 475	W/O Bailey	
9.7.43	9.30	HM 350	Sgt. Wilson	
18.7.43	08.45	DX 298	W/o Ward	
"	09.55	.	.	
6.8.43	10.10	P6262	Lt. Wangberg	
6.8.43	14.40	Z 7209	F/S Jacq	
10.8.43	13.50	HM 322	Sgt. Snell	
10.8.43	16.55	HM 350	Sgt. Cheatwin	
11.8.43	9.35	P6262	W/O Ward	

Extract from the diary of RAF Madley showing aircrew training schedules.

EFORDSHIRE.	Time carried forward :—		
		Flying Times	
REMARKS ncluding results of bombing, gunnery, exercises, etc.)		Day	Night
oming and Cf Sigs.		1·35	
ec. Tuning and Syko.		1·15	
No Ex.		1·20	
ec. Tuning and X Sigs.		1·30	
Homing and Cf Sigs.		1·15	
Tuning by Calib. — X Sigs.		1·25	
No Ex.		1·15	
Tuning by Calib. — X Sigs.		1·30	
No Ex.		1·30	
Tuning by Calib - Syko		1·35	
Homing & Q Sig.		1·25	
Simple Com		·55	
Freq chg by Bk Tuning		·50	
Freq. ch by bk tuning		1·05	
Simple Comms.		·25	
NX		·15	
Back tuning & fixes		1·15	
Back tuning & fixes		1·05	
Freq ch & homing		1·00	
Back tuning & fixes.		1·00	
Freq ch. & homing		1·05	
TOTAL TIME		24·30	

The final five months of the war saw no decline in the training schedule. With Bomber Command still applying enormous pressure by day as well as by night on the bombing of German cities and industrial targets, the aircraft losses continued. Only when victory finally came in May 1945 was the signal school allowed to relax. VE Day was celebrated in great style with jubilation going on until the small hours. It had been a job very well done. Although the intense pressure on Madley had eased, it was to remain a military airfield for the foreseeable future.

And what of Rudolph Hess? Hess had been appointed Hitler's deputy in 1932. A staunch Nazi, his loyalty to his leader was unfaltering and he agreed with Hitler that Britain was not Germany's natural enemy – it was Russia and the spread of Communism they despised. Imagining himself in the role of a peace envoy and without the consent of his Fuhrer, in 1941 Hess began to formulate the idea of flying to Britain to present Hitler's peace proposals in person. The one contact that he thought he had in the country was His Grace the 14th

A rare photograph of the crashed ME110 in which Hess flew to Scotland. (Origin unknown)

116

Duke of Hamilton and 11th Duke of Brandon who was the premier peer of Scotland. Hess said that he had met him at the 1936 Olympic Games held in Berlin, though the Duke always denied it. Nonetheless, Hess planned his flight for Saturday, 10 May 1941, writing a letter to Hitler to be opened four hours after his departure explaining his actions. At 2.30 pm on the 10th, he dressed in flying gear before climbing into a waiting Messerschmitt Bf110D and taking off on what he saw as a glorious mission for the Fatherland.

The flight successfully reached the Scottish mainland. Unfortunately finding nowhere flat to land and running out of fuel, Hess abandoned his aircraft to crash whilst he floated down on his parachute to land some distance from his intended target, Dungavel House, the home of the Duke. Landing heavily, Hess was apprehended by a local farmer, David McLean, and taken to McLean's farmhouse to await the military authorities.

Hess was moved under armed escort to the Home Guard Battalion headquarters in Giffnock and then to Maryhill Barracks in Glasgow where he was placed in a cell on his own. He was later transferred to the Drymen Military Hospital near Loch Lomond where his injuries were attended to and his 'state of mind' was assessed. An official announcement of his capture was broadcast by the BBC on 12th May. After further interrogation it was decided that Hess should be kept isolated and treated as a prisoner of war. He was put on a train for London under armed guard and whisked to the Tower of London, then later spent some months under psychiatric care at Mytchett Place near Aldershot in Hampshire, and finally, in June 1942, he was sent to Maindiff Court Hospital, Abergavenny, where he spent the next three years.

On 6 October 1945, orders were received that Hess was to be tried at Nuremberg. Four days later, accompanied by Major D. Ellis-Jones of the Royal Army Medical Corps, he arrived at Madley airfield prior to being flown to Brussels and then on to Nuremberg. A tight security cordon was thrown around the airfield as Hess was temporarily taken to the office in the control tower while arrangements were made for his flight. The senior air traffic controller at Madley, Flt Lt Tony Badman, was in charge of making these arrangments and allocated a Dominie for the first leg of the journey. With all the legal requirements satisfied, the aircraft left Madley at around 11.00 hrs to arrive in Brussels before lunch. Hess complained that it had been a rough flight and that he felt a little 'queasy'. Upon landing at Nuremberg, Hess was handed over to the relevant authorities.

Rudolph Hess. (After the Battle)

The International Military Tribunal opened on 20 November 1945 in the courtroom of the Palace of Justice. The trial dragged on until 30 September 1946 when judgement was finally delivered. While the Russians demanded the death penalty, the court ruled that Rudolph Hess should spend the rest of his life in Spandau Prison. This he did until his death in mysterious circumstances on 17 August 1987 at the age of 93.

Back at Madley, his departure in the Dominie had been welcomed by all. A high profile Nazi such as Hess had captured the world's headlines and had placed Madley into the history books. Many questions were, and continue to be, asked about his quest. The answers may never be known.

The role for Madley after those tumultuous days was that of a communications base. Many high profile VIPs were flown to various conferences both overseas and in the UK, giving the hope that Madley would have a long-term future. That, however, was not to be as the peacetime requirements of the RAF became less. By the 1950s the military had gone and most of the airfield had returned to agriculture. The siting of a British Telecom satellite tracking station within the

The BT satellite scanners now occupy part of Madley. (Author)

119

The very rare battle headquarters found at Madley. (Author)

Mike Stimson and his Stirling crew, 1944/5. Mike trained as a W/Op at Madley. (Mike Stimson)

airfield boundary with its huge dish aerials remained the only link with the air for some time to come. The land was farmed by the War Agricultural Organisation for many years after the Air Ministry had finished with it. Donald Parsons, whose land at Street House Farm was requisitioned in 1940 had first refusal to buy it back again between 1960 and 1965. He bought back the requisitioned land then sold it again. At the same time, Stone Street, which had been closed to the public during the war, was reopened.

Today, luckily, there are still some buildings to remind us of a very busy training station. The huge satellite dishes of BT remain and here and there one can find a wartime building now occupied by local engineering companies. The three rare Hinaidi hangars and the two Callender-Hamiltons are still standing and in use by various industries. They have withstood the ravages of time very well and are in reasonable condition. Amongst the various concrete buildings still *in situ* is the equally rare battle headquarters. Semi-sunk in the earth and built of bomb-proof concrete, this would have been brought into use had paratroopers invaded and landed at the airfield. From here, control of the defences and other airfield operations would have been conducted. It is still possible to enter via the hatch which opens into a three-roomed area and gives one an idea of how claustrophobic it would have been had it been necessary to bring it into use. The only natural light comes from the small slits built into the above-ground segment.

There are ghosts here. Perhaps they are those of the airmen who died whilst flying from the airfield. Enter the battle headquarters and you feel your neck tingle, a cold, clammy atmosphere envelops you and the silence is surreal. The remains of the runways still echo to the sound of aero engines of those far-off days.

A one-off occasion took place at Madley on Saturday, 21 May 2005 when a reunion was organised for the veterans who had trained and flown from the airfield. Organised by the Wetlands Study Centre, it brought together several hundred ex-RAF airmen and women in a day of reunion and celebration. The weather intervened and the scheduled flypast of a Dominie and Proctor aircraft could not take place, but this did not dampen the spirits of everyone there, as old friendships were renewed and new ones nurtured. Sadly, this event will not be repeated and for now, history is all we have left.

7
PERSHORE

The Vickers Wellington became known as one of the most outstanding aeroplanes of the war, which, due to its revolutionary 'geodetic' fuselage designed by Dr Barnes Wallis, could withstand terrific punishment. Known to all airmen as the 'Wimpey', it was the best of the twin-engined bombers. The prototype (K4049), powered by two 850 hp Bristol Pegasus X engines, first flew on 15 June 1936 with a production order being placed the same year.

It was a Wellington that made the first bombing attack of the war, on 4 September 1939 when a force attacked warships at Brunsduttel. Due to bad weather and heavy enemy fire, this first raid, during the course of which two aircraft were lost, was not a success. Further daylight raids also proved disastrous and from December 1939 the Wellington was used exclusively for night bombing. In this role it continued to give good service until the arrival of the four-engined heavy bombers. The Wellington, however, was not exclusively used in bombing Germany. Many found their way to the Operational Training Units (OTUs), including Pershore, one of the major wartime airfields in Worcestershire.

Known to some as Tilesford, the airfield lay two miles north-east of Pershore town and approximately seven miles from Worcester. Part of an estate belonging to Tilesford House, it was a large flat area of grassland which at the instigation of Mr R.J. Bunning was turned into an airfield in 1934 and, officially titled Throckmorton Airfield, became the home of the Worcestershire Flying School.

This was a period when civilian flying schools were beginning to flourish, possibly due to the fact that Alan Cobham, the aviation pioneer, was in the middle of his National Aviation Day Tours. The display first visited Worcester in September 1933, returning in June the

122

following year. For just five shillings any would-be aviator could take a flight in either an Avro 504 or one of the various de Havilland Moths that made up the fleet. Then there was the show itself, with a flypast of the aircraft before each one gave its own thrilling display to a huge crowd. Aerobatics, racing round pylons, wing walking and flour bombing were among the thrills, all intended to interest people in flying. And interest them it did, for within several months of opening, Worcester Flying School could boast around 120 members with at least 60 of them obtaining their licence fairly quickly. The club also operated a Civil Air Guard unit in which some would-be pilots could gain their licence for half the price charged by the flying club. They came not only from the immediate area but also from many of the West Midland towns and cities. Tilesford House became the clubhouse and played host to many social gatherings.

As interest in the club grew there came a requirement for hangarage. A corrugated shed with a workshop at one end was built with enough room to accommodate four de Havilland Moths. This scene of bliss continued until 1938 when once again the rumblings of war forced the Air Ministry Works Department to look at Pershore and it was approved for acquisition. Situated far from the battle front in the south of the country, it was to be classified as a training base along with several others in this area including Honeybourne, Moreton-in-Marsh and Defford.

In December 1940, all Bomber Command stations were being built to a standard pattern with two main runways extending to 1,400 yds (1,280 m) and the other two being 1,100 yds (1,000 m). By January 1941 the pattern was altered to one runway of 1,600 yds (1,460 m) capable of being extended to 2,000 yds (1,830 m) and the two secondary runways being 1,100 yds (1,000 m) with a possible extension to 1,400 yds (1,280 m). The latter was planned for Pershore and in early 1940 it fell to Messrs Wimpey and Co to turn the little flying club into a class 'A' bomber airfield.

Initially bad weather hampered progress but summer of that year saw three runways nearly complete together with four T2 hangars and a 'J' type hangar in various stages of construction. Technical and domestic blocks were built with the usual dispersed buildings such as the VHF/DF hut, and ammunition and bomb dumps hidden around the perimeter. All of this activity, however, did not go unnoticed by the Luftwaffe.

For some days, a lone enemy reconnaissance aircraft had been observed high over Pershore, the reason becoming clear on Wednesday,

The 'J' Type hangar, once the home of Wellington bombers, is still in good condition at Pershore. (Author)

11 September 1940. This was a day of high enemy activity in the south of the country due to the fact that Hitler was pressing for Operation *Seelöwe* (Sealion) to begin, the planned invasion of the UK. With the weather mainly fine but for some light cloud in the Channel during the 11th, major attacks had begun by the afternoon. It was early evening at Pershore when the unfamiliar drone of an aircraft was heard approaching. Most of the Wimpey workmen had gone home by then but the local villagers, mystified by the sound, came out of their houses to look up. They saw a solitary aircraft with a Balkan Cross under the wings and a Swastika on the tail approaching the airfield. Coming in low, the aircraft dropped two HE bombs. With a large explosion, some of the day's work on the airfield was demolished instantly, dust and flames rapidly covering a large area. It was the baptism of fire for the local populace.

That day was to prove bad for the Luftwaffe with 23 aircraft lost and a further 17 damaged. As if in retaliation, a return raid the next day delivered more devastation. Once again single aircraft were roaming around the West Midlands area when one spotted Pershore and dived low to deliver its deadly cargo. This time eleven HE and 100 incendiary bombs landed around the perimeter and in the adjacent fields. There was, however, no loss of human life in either raid although the second did kill some farm animals.

Parts of the airfield were now in ruins and efforts began to repair what had been damaged and to continue the building work. With the recent raid in mind, four concrete pillboxes were constructed around the perimeter. Two were situated on the western approach to the airfield with the remaining two alongside the approach road. Work was allowed to continue unhindered by further raids for the rest of the year and by early 1941, completion was in sight. However, on 6 February FO W.J.R. Warren arrived with the advance party to find the airfield both muddy, untidy and far from finished. Three weeks later the Senior Administration Officer, Sqd Ldr R.A. Williams, found it in a similar state. Determined to get the airfield operational as soon as possible, threats to the workforce by the temporary CO, Wg Cdr L.E. Jarman, DFC, worked wonders although by the time the first aircraft arrived in April, it still was not completely finished.

With the arrival of the appointed CO, Gp Capt J.R.W. Smyth-Pigott, DSO and Bar, on 1 April 1941, Pershore was encompassed within No 6 Group of Bomber Command which had its headquarters at RAF Abingdon in Oxfordshire. Notice was also given that it was to become the home of No 23 OTU responsible for the training of Canadian crews for the new Commonwealth squadrons of the RAF. By sheer coincidence, this activity heralded the return of the Luftwaffe. Sunday, 10 March 1941 dawned foggy over most of the Midlands and it was not until the evening that the skies began to clear. On the other side of the Channel, *Luftflotten* 2 and 3 were anxious to become airborne but could not do so until the fog lifted. In the event it was only aircraft of the latter unit that did eventually get the signal that a raid was on. In all, 184 German bombers left their French airfields by 21.30 hrs with orders to bomb the Bristol area. Whilst the majority of the enemy aircraft found the target, several drifted towards the West Midlands.

At 22.25 hrs, a pattern of 16 HE bombs rained down on Pershore. In seconds the Motor Transport (MT) yard became a mass of flames whilst some bombs fell outside the airfield perimeter. At that time of night and with the airfield not yet fully operational there were few personnel on site and there was no loss of life, but several vehicles were destroyed and clearance of the debris was to take several weeks.

Most of the repair work was completed by 1st April when the first of the aircraft arrived. The Vickers Wellington Ic was to become the workhorse of many of the OTUs including No 23. Coded BY and FZ respectively, they were joined by an Avro Anson and later in the year, a Tiger Moth was on strength and used in a communications role.

Ten days later it appeared as though the enemy reconnaissance flights had done their job well when Pershore was visited once again by the Luftwaffe. The night of Thursday, 10/11 April saw devastating raids all over the West Midlands with Birmingham being the main target. At 00.35 hrs, a lone Ju 88, with the help of a full moon, noticed the uncamouflaged runways. Running in at 3,000 ft, two HE bombs were dropped. This time the aiming was good as two petrol bowsers full of aviation fuel exploded. The fire crews were soon in action but despite their pouring foam over what remained of the vehicles, they found containment difficult as fuel running down the drains constantly burst into flames. A second casualty of the attack was one of the Wellingtons parked alongside the main runway. Though not destroyed, it was severely damaged by the second bomb which landed nearby. Again, fortunately no one was killed but the destruction did delay the completion date for the airfield handover. The county itself, however, suffered badly with ten separate incidents reported, some very serious.

The rest of the month was spent in relative calm as the OTU got itself onto an operational footing. The arrival of the military in what was a very agricultural area brought its own rewards when three local farmers, Mr Meekie, Mr Boswell and Mr Knight started a pig farm and market garden to supply fresh meat and produce to the camp. With rationing the bugbear of most civilians, personnel at Pershore had no such problems.

However, it was the arrival of a Miles Martinet tug towing aircraft that brought full operational status a little closer. This was the first aircraft to enter service with the RAF to be designed from the outset as a pure target tug. When production finished in 1945, a total of 1,724 had been built. The single aircraft attached to 23 OTU was assigned to target towing with the additional duty of fighter affiliation training.

May saw a return of the Luftwaffe when the night of the 9th/10th brought far-ranging attacks in which 89 long-range bombers and 19 long-range fighter/bombers were engaged. With aircraft roaming all over the Midlands, the searchlight battery at Upton Snodsbury illuminated an He 111. From the noise of engines it was obvious that several other aircraft were in the vicinity. Shortly after midnight, two

HE bombs were dropped close to the airfield with a further two ten minutes later. Five minutes had passed when the same aircraft flew across the airfield. As it did so the defence posts opened fire and although it appeared as though hits had been registered, the He 111 continued to fly straight and level until it disappeared into cloud. On this occasion, no bombs were dropped on Pershore.

The next night once more saw a lot of activity in the area. Searchlights were again illuminating aircraft, one in particular being an He 111H-8 (3971) of KG55. This was caught by No 380 Searchlight Unit and held, allowing the nearby anti-aircraft guns to get in several hits. Mortally wounded, the aircraft finally crashed at Rumbush Farm, Earlswood near Birmingham. Coded GI+EM, it had a crew of four and Oblt Johannes Speck von Sternberg (*Staffelkapitan-pilot*), Fw F. Muhn (obs) and Fw S. Ruhel (flt eng) were all killed. The only survivor was Gefr Rudolph Budde (w/op) who was thrown into a ditch by the impact of the crash with his clothes on fire. Though badly burnt, he survived to become a POW.

With the arrival of further Wellingtons throughout April and into May, training got under way. This consisted of ground bombing instruction, gunnery instruction, wireless procedures, navigation, dinghy drill and pilot training. All of this had to be studied and exams passed before the trainees got airborne in the Wellingtons. When they did so the aircraft usually carried three trainees from each trade in order to maximise the use of the aircraft and also to ensure that the output of trained aircrew was at peak level. Right from the beginning the OTUs were to experience appalling losses, No 23 being no exception. As the training increased in intensity, so did the accidents.

On the morning of 2nd June, Wellington R1662 was prepared for a cross-country sortie under the captaincy of Flt Lt B.R. Ker. With a trainee pilot at the controls, the take-off and initial flight were fine. One hour into the exercise, the aircraft suddenly dropped to the right. Flt Lt Ker immediately took control but with the port engine giving very little power, he decided to crash-land in a clearing he could see just ahead. The crew braced themselves as the Wellington ploughed into the ground. Earth and debris flew everywhere, as it slid along the wet grass and with a crunching sound, accompanied by the noise of tearing metal, one wing was torn off by a tree. As the aircraft finally slewed to a halt, fire broke out at the back. The rest of the crew made it safely out, but Sgt K.J. Kellough of the RCAF found he was trapped in the tail gun position with a broken leg. Despite efforts by the rest of the crew to get him out, the flames became too intense and beat them back.

Repair and cleaning of a Wellington of No 15 OTU, a scene repeated at Pershore with No 23 OTU. (Imperial War Museum)

It was not until the arrival of the fire tender which finally put the flames out that it was possible to extricate Sgt Kellough from the turret. Still alive, he was rushed to Doncaster Infirmary but sadly died of his injuries some hours later.

With a full complement of aircraft and with training gathering momentum, it was found that Pershore was in need of a satellite airfield. Defford, just a few miles away, was chosen and although construction had already begun, it was a long way behind schedule.

Now a very cosmopolitan unit with trainee aircrew arriving from the RNZAF and RAAF as well as the RCAF and the RAF, the first real operation came on the night of 20/21 July when a leaflet dropping sortie (or 'nickelling' as it was known) was carried out. Six Wellingtons from 'C' Flight were prepared during the afternoon and with good visibility over the target forecast, the first aircraft (R1803) flown by FO Morton, took off at 23.00 hrs followed by the other five leaving at two minute intervals. With the target easily located, 73 packages of leaflets were dropped. In addition, each aircraft was carrying two 250lb bombs, and these were dropped on enemy-held airfields within the same area. Wellington X9631, captained by Sqd Ldr Ker (he of the crash-landing), found difficulty in releasing his bomb load and finally jettisoned them over the Channel.

All six aircraft made it back to the English coastline, but X9659 flown by the now Chief Instructor, Wg Cdr Jarman, caught a balloon cable which caused a partial failure in one of the engines. Nursing his aircraft along, he managed to land safely at Pershore. The first real mission for 23 OTU had been a success. As July 1941 came to an end the unit had achieved 1,312 hours flying by day and 683 hours by night. No mean achievement considering the disruption of flying from an unfinished airfield. The same problem at Defford had prevented the OTU from using its facilities, a situation that was to continue until September when finally construction was finished.

There were many high and low points for the OTUs. An inspection by the Inspector General, Air Chief Marshal Sir Arthur Longmore, GCB, DSO, on 13th August was somewhat overshadowed by events that took place shortly after his departure from Pershore. That morning, Wellington X9654 had been prepared for a sortie to practise landings using wireless procedures. This was to be a low level flight to nearby RAF Abingdon. With an eight-man crew consisting of PO H.G. Pilling, PO E.D. Baker (RCAF), Sgt A.H. Harris (RCAF), Sgt L. West, Sgt G.J. Kearns (RCAF), Sgt W.H. Bracken (RCAF), Sgt S.W. Griffin and Sgt L.C. Young, the aircraft left Pershore shortly after the ACM's arrival. Reaching Abingdon at around 15.00 hrs, it had turned onto its final approach when a malfunction in the flap system caused the Wellington to stall at 30 ft and crash near the runway where it caught fire. Harris, West and Griffin were taken to the Radcliffe Infirmary whilst Sgt Young was treated at Abingdon. The rest of the crew suffered minor cuts and bruises but while they all survived this crash, within less than a year they were all to perish on bombing operations.

Meanwhile, 'nickelling' operations gave the crews their first taste of operational flying. 17th August saw the next sortie when once again six Wellingtons were despatched to the Paris area. The leaflets dropped explained to the French the aims of the Anglo-American Declaration of War and were intended to reassure the people that victory would soon be achieved. For the occupying forces, they became a source of toilet paper!

By late 1941 the losses experienced by Bomber Command were becoming colossal. With pressure on the OTUs to pass aircrew faster, the type of training became demanding in the extreme. Every fine day would see flying in the morning followed by classroom in the afternoon. If the weather closed in it was classroom both morning and afternoon. The occasional 'nickelling' sortie at night was followed by further cross-country exercises and more classroom training. One element not left to bureaucracy at the OTUs was the cohesion of crews. No special selection of a crew took place: it was just a natural process of self-selection. Someone wanted a gunner or a wireless operator. What about him over there? Looks as if he could fit in. Talking to each other they found a common bond thus eliminating as far as possible a clash of personalities that might further endanger an already dangerous occupation. By this process, complete and compatible crews were born.

In addition to learning flying skills at Pershore, the trainees undertook fighter affiliation exercises. These were carried out in conjunction with a Ground Controlled Interception (GCI) station at nearby Comberton. The Wellingtons on cross-country exercises would be intercepted by fighter units which had been directed towards them by Comberton. This gave the trainee gunners practice at sighting approaching enemy fighters, a skill that they would all too soon be putting into use under the most dangerous conditions.

September was at last to see the completion of the satellite at Defford. Lying three miles to the south-west of Pershore town, it gave an uninterrupted view across the Malvern Hills. Its completion was to ease the congestion at Pershore for only a limited time. The Ministry of Aircraft Production had other ideas for the satellite.

Back at Pershore, another leaflet operation was scheduled for 20th October using aircraft from 'C' and 'D' flights. The target once more was the Paris area with orders to bomb enemy airfields again. Six aircraft left Pershore at 18.43 hrs including Wellington 'Q' (Z8786) flown by Fl Lt R.J. Newton with an all-NCO crew consisting of FS Cooper, Sgt F.A. Tait (RCAF), Sgt H. Smith, Sgt P.N. Herbert, Sgt Harrison, Sgt H.F. Farley and Sgt G.T. Ramm. The leaflets were dropped successfully but not so the bomb load. Warning the crew that they would have to bring the bombs back, the captain turned for home. Halfway across the Channel a further problem occurred when the intercom system failed. Reaching Pershore and turning onto a final approach, the Wellington crashed just short of the runway at 23.17 hrs. Immediately the port engine caught fire, a blaze that rapidly engulfed the entire aircraft. Despite this the crew were able to scramble to safety just before the ammunition and bombs exploded, sending small pieces of red-hot shrapnel through the air. Several members of the fire crew sustained injuries and were treated in the sick quarters at Pershore. It took several hours for the fire to die down whereupon clearance of the wreckage could begin.

Six days later a tragedy occurred that affected everyone at Pershore. It was normal practice to carry out an air test during the afternoon before every night operation. This was to make sure the aircraft was functioning correctly and all major systems were working before it was signed over to its crew. During the afternoon of the 6th, aircraft from 'C' and 'D flights were air tested prior to a night 'nickelling' operation. Wellington Ic, T2844, was one of those aircraft. The crew, PO H. Rose, Sgt T.N.D. Boyd (RCAF), PO M.F. Gibson (RCAF), FS W. Walker, PO R.C. Symes, Sgt F.H.P. Tolley and Sgt P.E. Lacey (RCAF) boarded the aircraft at 16.45 hrs. The take-off was normal but some 15 minutes into the flight the dinghy broke loose and began to self-inflate within the cabin. In doing so it fouled the aircraft controls causing a non-recoverable dive. As this became steeper, both mainplanes failed and with a terrifying scream, the Wellington ploughed into the ground four miles north-northwest of Cheltenham. There were sadly no survivors. By the time the crash tender, fire crew and ambulances arrived very little of the aircraft was distinguishable. The three Commonwealth airmen were taken to Gloucester Old Cemetery whilst the others were taken for private burial. Such was the shock to the station of this tragic accident that the night operation was promptly cancelled.

With the end of 1941 fast approaching it was time to look back at the past twelve months. It had been an eventful year for 23 OTU with some success and some tragedy. 1941 had cost the bomber OTUs around 400 aircraft, of which 350 losses were caused by training mishaps. This could be because of various factors, with bad weather playing a big part and mechanical failure and trainee errors also making a contribution.

Now, with 1942 about to dawn, morale low and poor bombing results, the state of Bomber Command appeared to be at its lowest. It was necessary to rethink the entire structure of the chain of command. In January 1942, the then-C-in-C, Air Marshal Sir Richard Pierce was moved from HQ Bomber Command at High Wycombe to be replaced by the formidable Air Chief Marshal Arthur Harris. Those bad fortunes were about to change.

Christmas 1941 had been celebrated at Pershore in the usual fashion, with a period of rest until the new year. January got off to a very bad start. The 3rd once again saw the loss of an entire crew when Wellington Ic T2953 crashed into a thickly wooded area to the west of the airfield at 19.00 hrs. Weather conditions were bad with low cloud and drizzle at the time, having deteriorated since take-off. It was a training exercise to practise circuits and landings with the crash occurring whilst the pilot was attempting to line up with the runway. The five-man crew comprised a screened pilot, two pupil pilots and two wireless operators. Sgts F.B. Murphy and B.B. Connel of the Royal Australian Air Force were laid to rest in Pershore cemetery whilst PO R.P. Hay, Sgt J.H. Marshall and Sgt H.K. Jones were taken for private burials.

The month of January was to see a further fatality when Wellington Ic R1803 lost engine power whilst attempting an overshoot at Pershore. The crash caused the fuselage to break in half, scattering wreckage over a vast area. Sgt J.H. Bye (RCAF) was killed, reported to have fallen from the aircraft just prior to the impact. Although injured, the pilot, Sgt I.D. Steward and Sgt P.E. Poulson survived with Sgt W.Clayton, Sgt F.G. Forbes (RCAF) and Sgt W.L. Kellow receiving bad bruising.

Situated as it was in the middle of the country, Pershore often received visitors in the form of aircraft either lost or having difficulty in reaching their own bases when returning from a raid. During 1941 Hampdens and Stirlings had been glad to find a safe haven at Pershore but one of the more unusual types to land was an Avro Manchester on 10th January. The forerunner to the Lancaster, the Manchester suffered a brief and unfortunate service life due to its under-developed and unreliable Rolls-Royce Vulture engines. The aircraft that landed at

Pershore, L7476, had flown to the enemy-held port of Brest hoping to bomb the battle cruisers in port. Due to bad visibility the crew had aborted the mission and landed at Pershore when low on fuel.

With the new year came a change in commanding officer at Pershore. The departure of Gp Cpt Smyth-Pigott had brought a temporary CO in the form of Wg Cdr J.A. Roncaroni. He remained in command for three days until Gp Cpt A.R. Coombe assumed command at a crucial time for the OTU. The satellite at Defford was being taken over by the Ministry of Aircraft Production and no replacement was forthcoming, severely restricting the training programme.

Perhaps one of the most unusual sorties carried out by the OTU took place during April. It was prompted by the Luftwaffe's *Baedeker* raids, so called because the targets were all cities listed in the *Baedeker* tourist guides. One such raid was on the Georgian city of Bath when on the night of 25/26 April, 92 tonnes of bombs were dropped on the city centre, causing heavy casualties and extensive damage. The next night another raid culminated over Bath when 43 tonnes of bombs landed on the city. In this case however, a high wind accelerated the spread of fire which took days to dampen down. Casualties were high with the two raids leaving 401 dead, 357 seriously injured and 515 slightly wounded. The next morning a signal was received at Pershore requesting a Wellington of 'D' flight be sent to take photographs of the bombed city. Only from the air could the true extent of damage be seen. When the photographs were developed and placed together to form a montage of the city it became apparent that these had been devastating raids.

Training continued until the end of the month unfortunately with further tragedies. Wellington R1597 crashed in the Brecon Beacons with the total loss of all seven crew while in another incident the crew of R1618 were injured but managed to survive.

Harris was now firmly in the top seat of Bomber Command, and one of the first proposals to reach him was to consider the saturation bombing of 20 German cities. Since his arrival in February, the maximum number of aircraft sent on one bombing raid had been around 250. With these new proposals came the suggestion of sending 1,000 bombers to a designated German city. This figure could only be reached by including aircraft from the Reserve and OTUs. Planning went ahead and it was decided that the city of Cologne would receive the first 1,000 bomber raid over the night of 30/31 May 1942.

The most westerly OTU briefed to take part in the attack was Pershore. It would contribute 34 aircraft with some of them operating

Air Chief Marshal Sir Arthur 'Bomber' Harris, C-in-C Bomber Command 1942–1945. (Imperial War Museum)

Home but broken – a warrior returns. (Bomber Command)

from Stradishall, Bourne and Oakington. These would form part of the huge bombing force comprising 602 Wellingtons, 88 Stirlings, 131 Halifaxes, 28 Whitleys, 46 Manchesters, 73 Lancasters and 79 Hampdens, a total of 1,047 aircraft. Days before the raid a security cordon was thrown around Pershore and all the other bases. No one was allowed out and only with a special pass could anyone get on the airfield.

The forecast for 30/31 May was not reassuring with light cloud expected over Cologne. There would be thick cloud along the route, which was predicted to clear on the return leg. At the C-in-C's office at High Wycombe, the Senior Air Staff Officer, Air Vice-Marshal R H Saundby, was speaking to the command radar officer, Wg Cdr Dudley Saward.

'What's going to happen with this raid?' asked Saward. 'Is it going to be okay?'

'I hope so,' replied Saundby. 'I expect it will be. The C-in-C always has the luck of the Devil!'

At Pershore work on the aircraft continued all day. They were armed, bombed up and fuelled. The afternoon air tests went well and by the time the 19 crews went to the briefing, the aircraft were ready and waiting. At 18.00 hrs, the doors of the briefing room were locked and an armed guard placed outside. The windows had been blacked out and on the raised platform stood the Station Commander, the OTU Commander and other senior officers. Reaching up, the CO pulled the cover off a large map of Europe, saying 'Gentlemen. The target for tonight is Cologne.' After the main briefing for the raid, code-named 'Trout' due to the fact that Harris was a keen angler, a message was read out from the C-in-C himself. It stated the historic nature of the raid and finished by wishing all the crews good luck. Next came the briefings by the armament, navigation, flying control, meteorological and signals officers. Last to speak was Gp Cpt Smyth-Pigott who emphasised that this raid was to be a maximum effort by Bomber Command and if successful, could help to shorten the war.

As they left the room, each man had his own thoughts. What would the flak be like? What about night-fighters? Would they all get back or would they be shot down to lie in some foreign field? Some hours before they had all written their letters to loved ones should they not come back. It was now back to their beds for a few hours before they boarded the trucks to take them to the aircraft waiting at dispersal, many feeling sick at this, their first real mission. It was an anxious time until the take-off when all thoughts would be concentrated on the mission.

The intended time over the target was 01.05 to 02.20 hrs. With Pershore situated in the middle of the country, some of the aircraft from 23 OTU would have at least one hour's flying time before they joined the main formation assembling over the Suffolk coastline. By 22.30 hrs the aircraft were taking off and looking ahead for the main force. Once they had joined the bomber stream they crossed the North Sea and approached the Dutch coast. Immediately the flak began to come up from the land and the flak ships anchored just off shore. The exploding shells were throwing shrapnel everywhere, creating fear that the flak would hit a vulnerable part of the aircraft and send it to its doom. The searchlights were roaming the sky, illuminating the aircraft as bright as day.

For one of the Wellingtons, N28561, it was not the flak that caused a problem but an unseen enemy night-fighter. The Wellington had taken off from Stradishall at 23.12 hrs and was flown by FS W.R.C. Johnson (RCAF). It was shot down at ten minutes past midnight near Gravendeel in Holland, killing the entire NCO crew of Sgt J. Donn-

Patterson (RAAF), Sgt M.L. Glenton-Wright (RAAF), Sgt G.F. Bolton (RAAF) and Sgt R.A. Broodbank (RAAF).

Battling against further flak, searchlights and enemy aircraft, the rest of the bombers approached Cologne at varying heights above the target. The first fires in the city became plain to see.

By the time 23 OTU arrived over the target, the city was ablaze. Dropping their bombs accurately from between 9,000 ft and 14,000 ft then turning for home, the fires could be seen for many miles as they left the carnage behind. The city was reduced to rubble with 460 dead, 59,000 homeless and 18,000 buildings destroyed. As the first light of dawn appeared on the horizon, the Wellingtons approached Pershore. The first aircraft to land was Wellington AD628, the rest following at differing intervals. Sadly, the loss of FS Johnson and his crew marred an otherwise successful operation, the first for all the crews. A reconnaissance flight over Cologne shortly after dawn reported the city in ruins. 23 OTU had played their part and a signal from the C-in-C congratulating them was received at Pershore the next day. Some weeks later leaflets were dropped in the major cities of the Ruhr stating that 'Cologne was proof of the growing power of the British Bomber Force'. It also warned of what Germany would receive, city by city, from now on.

That threat came true over the night of 1/2 June when the target was Essen. For this operation Pershore sent 33 Wellingtons – still without a satellite and using the same airfields as they had for Cologne. 956 aircraft were despatched this time. The weather over the target was disappointing and many crews had difficulty in finding the target, causing bombing to be very scattered. The OTU sadly lost two entire crews on the outbound journey when Wellingtons R1266 and Z8869 crashed in Holland. The victims of enemy night-fighters, both crews were buried in Holland. On this one operation, Bomber Command lost 31 aircraft.

The OTU went back to its training routine, sadly in the process losing a further two aircraft. Wellington X3172 had left Pershore for a dawn cross-country training exercise when, 15 minutes into the flight, a propeller came off. Attempting to call Pershore on the radio, the pilot lost sight of the airfield and losing height, crash-landed short of the perimeter, luckily with no loss of life. Two days later an entire crew was lost when the dinghy broke loose in L7891 and fouled the controls. FS C.G. McDonald (RCAF), PO C.D. Chant, PO A.W. Smith, PO L.G. Morrison (RCAF) and Sgt F.W. Sims were killed when the aircraft crashed eight miles east-southeast of Oxford.

With the moon entering a new phase, the opportunities to carry out further large scale raids were becoming fewer. However, another '1,000' raid was planned for the night of 25/26 June with the target this time being Bremen. Once again a veil of secrecy was thrown around Pershore with briefing carried out in locked huts. This time the 17 aircraft of the OTU were operating from Pershore, with a take-off time of 22.30 hrs.

Despite a reasonable weather forecast, Bremen was found to be covered in cloud making accurate bombing difficult. On this occasion, however, the leading aircraft were using Gee, a navigational aid to help pinpoint targets in bad conditions. This enabled the first wave of bombers to drop their bombs around the city centre causing an instant fireball which the later crews were able to see. The return journey was to prove difficult with intense flak, many searchlights and enemy aircraft. Two Wellingtons of the OTU did not return, both lost with their entire crews. Wellington DV475 was shot down by Oblt Werner Rowlin of 111/NJG1 whilst X9875 was presumed lost over the coast of Holland. On this raid, the heaviest casualties were suffered by the OTUs of 91 Group. Of the 198 Whitleys and Wellingtons that flew that night, 23 did not return.

Bremen was the last '1,000' bomber raid in which 23 OTU would participate. Further sorties to Germany were carried out, however, such as the raid on Dusseldorf over the night of 31 July/1 August in which seven aircraft from Pershore took part. One Wellington, X9917, failed to return but all the crew managed to bale out, becoming POWs.

The rest of the year was taken up mainly with further training incorporating cross-country flights and the inevitable 'Bullseye' night exercises. The arrival of the WAAFs on 28 June was welcomed by all the men even though their accommodation was approximately half a mile away near the village of Pinvin. But even the girls could not raise the morale when 1942 ended with several further accidents involving loss of life. September was to prove a bad month when three Wellingtons were lost over the night of 16th/17th. A force of 369 aircraft destined for another raid on Essen and in particular the Krupps Engineering works was joined by 14 from Pershore. Taking off around 20.00 hrs, the three that failed to return were all new versions of the Wellington, the Mark III. Z1730, B3720 and X3799 were lost with a total of 13 crew members, 2 being taken prisoner. This raid, however, did mark the end of the OTU's involvement in main operations. The record shows that over eight sorties to Germany, nine aircraft from 23 OTU were lost.

Towards the end of 1942 RAF Wellesbourne Mountford was designated a satellite to Pershore. Almost immediately and due to the overcrowding at the parent airfield, 'A' Flight was detached there. The airfield was used mainly for circuit and landing exercises but the speed of the training necessitated another satellite being allocated, this time RAF Atherstone which became the home of 'B' Flight. With the devastating losses being suffered by Bomber Command at this juncture of the war, the training programme was again accelerated. Crews were emerging from the OTUs in ever increasing numbers and with less training. In order to help the programme, 23 OTU were allocated a number of Wellington Mk III aircraft, which were gradually replacing the older Mk Is in the command.

The last days of December saw one of the new marks crash when BK517, on a mid-morning air test, encountered bad weather conditions which resulted in the aircraft coming down in trees near Banbury in Oxfordshire. The crew, FO J.G. Bryne, FS J.T. McDonald (RCAF), FS W. McMillan, LAC L.H. Nicholson, AC2 J.E.G. Beaumont and AC2 G. Broadhurst were killed. It was a sad ending to a year of very mixed fortunes.

With the training programme once again accelerated, January 1943 began with the usual cross country flying exercises punctuated with the occasional 'nickelling' operation. On 12th January, five aircraft were detailed to carry out such an operation over the Nantes area of France. Although the weather was far from ideal, all aircraft returned safely. Not so on the training exercise three days later when two Wellingtons crashed within hours of each other. With a take-off time of 18.00 hrs, Wellington BK512 left Pershore for a 'Bullseye' exercise armed with practice bombs. One hour into the sortie the starboard engine seized up over Orton-on-the-Hill in Leicestershire. Ordering his crew to bale out, FO A.M.H. Gain (RCAF) struggled to maintain height whilst looking for a place to crash-land. Sadly the aircraft dropped and he crashed to his death. The rest of the crew parachuted to safety. Some hours later X3964 took off for a night circuit training exercise. All went well until 21.55 hrs, when an engine cut after the centre cam-shaft roller bearing disintegated in the port engine. With only 200 ft in hand, the pilot crashed into the ground short of the runway. All three crew – FS W.J.A. Duplin (RCAF), and Sgts J.H. Robson and W.E. Barr (RCAF) – perished in the ensuing fire.

Though not taking part in the Berlin raid on the night of 17/18 January, nine aircraft from the OTU were tasked with searching for aircrew lost whilst returning from the raid. Covering the North Sea,

The final resting place for many Canadian and Australian aircrew who died whilst flying from Pershore. (Author)

the crews searched for several hours looking for dinghies without any success. An observer in one of the aircraft taking part (though not from Pershore) was the broadcaster Richard Dimbleby. He flew in a Lancaster of No 106 Squadron piloted by Wg Cdr Guy Gibson. When returned safely to Syerston, his recorded radio broadcast several days later relayed to the listeners the terrors of bombing Germany.

Many British aircraft became victims of friendly fire. An incident on 26th January may well have been such a case. Wellington III Z1695 took off from Pershore on a 'Bullseye' sortie. Crewed by Sgt J.S. Cornfield (RCAF), PO R.P. Love, Sgt T.A.J. Whalley, Sgt B.P. Enright, FO D.R.A. MacDougal (RCAF) and Sgt J.J. Snyden (RCAF), the aircraft was flying over Yarmouth when it was caught in a searchlight beam. As this occurred, flames were seen to appear over the wings, quickly spreading to the fuselage. In seconds the tail unit broke away and the rest of the aircraft dived and crashed with a loud explosion into Runham Marches near Yarmouth. No one survived the impact and no explanation has ever been found or put forward as to what caused the fire.

Pilots of the ATA. (Imperial War Museum)

It was another sad occasion for 23 OTU, which was further accentuated when two Wellingtons of the unit collided in cloud with the loss of two good crews. Later that day yet another aircraft, BK503, lost power and crashed near Worcester losing two crew members and injuring a further three. The coming months of 1943 saw many more aircraft downed with crews losing their lives or suffering dreadful injury. They are too numerous to mention every incident but the aforementioned will indicate the dangers inherent at this period of the war. One only has to visit Pershore Cemetery to find a total of 57 Canadians buried within the grounds, just a few of the lives lost from No 23 OTU.

The rest of the year and early 1944 were to see a continuation of training interspersed with the occasional 'nickel' operation. Rumours had abounded for some time that the unit was to be amalgamated with another OTU as Bomber Command gained superiority of the air over Germany, losses became fewer and the pressure eased on the number of crews required. The rumours became fact in April 1944 when

The smiling face of a ferry pilot of the ATA. (Crown)

23 OTU was disbanded and absorbed into 22 OTU at the satellite airfield of Wellesbourne Mountford. One month later saw Gp Cpt M.D. Crichton-Biggie, DFC, replace Gp Cpt Combe as CO as Pershore prepared for its new role as No 1 Ferry Unit.

Before the war it had been the duty of all RAF squadrons to collect their own aircraft from the factories and repair facilities. With the outbreak of hostilities this system clearly could not continue and gave way to the forming of the Air Transport Auxiliary. This new unit incorporated both civilian and military pilots and groundcrews but it was the latter that became No 1 Ferry Unit, tasked with the collection of aircraft from factories. The groundcrews at Pershore would then check them out before the aircrews finally flew them overseas.

In 1940 when it was formed, the Air Transport Auxiliary was attached to BOAC as the majority of pilots who volunteered were privately or commercially trained. Later it was to come under 41 Group, Maintenance Command. From 1944, Pershore was to see various types of aircraft including Mosquitos, Beaufighters, Halifaxes

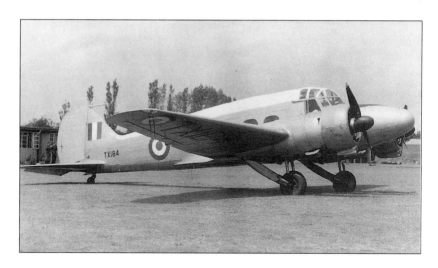

The Avro Anson, known as 'Faithful Annie' and used by most of the OTUs and Ferry Command. (MAP)

Some of the post-war work carried out at Pershore was on Canberra jet aircraft. (QinetiQ)

and Venturas, the majority of them being ferried oversees. The normal routine was that once the aircraft had been collected and checked over at Pershore, the crews would fly them down to Portreath or St Mawgan in Cornwall where they would be refuelled before being flown to their final destination. In the early months of 1944 this flying was done mainly at night but as the end of the war approached, daytime flying became the norm.

The unit did sterling work whilst at Pershore. May 1944 saw 1,556 hours flown when 138 aircraft were despatched overseas. During August 1944 five crews left Pershore flying Avro Ansons. After making

Pershore airfield, still preserved today. (QinetiQ)

145

a stop at Broadwell airfield in Oxfordshire, they flew on to Normandy Strip 24 to deliver the aircraft for use in Europe. September saw 192 aircraft delivered, a record for the unit. Gp Cpt R.S. Ryan arrived to command No 1 Ferry Unit in December 1944, a position he was to hold as the last days of war approached. When the conflict did end in May 1945, Pershore, along with the rest of the RAF, celebrated Victory in Europe.

The Ferry unit was to continue at Pershore until 1948 when it moved to Manston in Kent, having delivered thousands of aircraft worldwide. The airfield now became the home of the RAF Police Training School as well as seeing the arrival of the jet age in 1948. Part of the site was leased to Gloster Aircraft Company for secret flying trials with the Meteor, Canberra and later the Javelin.

With the outbreak of the Korean War in 1950, Pershore once again became a training school when No 10 AFS, under the command of Gp Cpt G.R. Howie, DSO, formed at the airfield. In the end they were not required and just as local people had become used to the sound of the twin-engine Airspeed Oxfords above their houses, the school closed in April 1954. It was, however, not the end of flying at Pershore.

Pershore's type 13726/41 control tower with peacetime glass addition. (Author)

September 1957 saw the Royal Radar Establishments Flying Unit take up residence having flown in from nearby Defford, one-time satellite to Pershore. This was a unit tasked with providing support for the radar establishment sited at Malvern, a place long associated with telecommunications. It used a variety of aircraft, some of which were jet powered, and the runway had to be extended to accommodate these. With bridleways and footpaths having to be closed, the extension was to prove very controversial. The local people, fearing an increase in noise and flying activity, protested at every opportunity but to no avail. A period of secrecy once again enveloped Pershore when around this time trials were carried out in radar techniques.

With the runway now lengthened to 2,450 yds, the airfield was capable of handling any of the jet aircraft of the period. Another user of Pershore in these latter days was the Defford Aero Club. They began by flying Tiger Moths but by 1977 had stopped power flying in favour of gliders.

1960 saw the dispersal at Pershore of large 'V' bombers such as the Valiant and Vulcan. These were part of Strike Command and were on permanent standby. Dispersed on the Bishampton side of the airfield, they could be scrambled in a number of minutes should the need arise. However, by 1972 no aircraft remained as the base began to be run down. The reason given for its closure was that with four radar experimental flying stations open, one had to go. Unfortunately that one was Pershore, leaving Bedford, Farnborough and Boscombe Down to continue the research. In 1978 the site was placed under Care and Maintenance and the memories of so many were confined to the history books. Many aircrew had learnt their skills at Pershore before moving on to operational squadrons and contributing to the defeat of the enemy. It was thus assured of its place in the history of the Second World War.

This was not, however, the end for Pershore. In 1981 the airfield was used by the Royal Signals for research into future radar techniques. It was taken over by the MOD and a privatised company called QinetiQ is now the user. Security is still intense as instruction is given here to chauffeurs who will drive top diplomats around the various trouble spots of this modern world. Where many aircraft types once sped down the runway, fast, high-powered cars have replaced them. The airfield is superbly preserved with hangars, control tower and many other wartime buildings still intact. As the main wartime operational airfield within the area, let us hope it remains as a memorial to all those who died or served at Pershore.

8
SHOBDON

It is fair to say that without the Glider Pilot Regiment, D-Day and all the other airborne operations of the war would have proved a harder task or at worst, they might have failed entirely. The men that made up the Regiment, soldiers trained in combat skills as well as flying, were to become known as 'total soldiers'. They were all volunteers from the RAF and various army regiments. They underwent the same selection process as normal RAF aircrew recruits before moving on to an Elementary Flying Training School (EFTS) for flying instruction on Tiger Moths. From this they proceeded to a Glider Training School to learn to fly General Aircraft Hotspur gliders. One such school was situated in a rural part of Herefordshire and went under the name of Shobdon.

Originally known as Pembridge Landing Ground, the site is on the B4362, a minor road close to the village of Shobdon. Farmland belonging to Broomlands Farm had been requisitioned when hostilities began but in 1940 the site only supported occasional army manoeuvres. One year later with the need for a training airfield far from the main battle area , Shobdon was put forward for development. It was situated between the Rivers Arrow and Lugg on a very flat plain with few roads or buildings and surrounded by the natural camouflage of woodland.

The contractors, together with the local farmworkers, moved in to clear hedges and obstructions. One problem discovered early on was the lack of a suitable water supply. The River Arrow was not large enough to sustain a major camp but it was felt that the Lugg was. The proposal was therefore made to move the planned airfield further north to enable a pipeline from the Lugg to be put in.

Although naturally camouflaged by trees, it was thought the airfield once built could become a target for the Luftwaffe. It was therefore

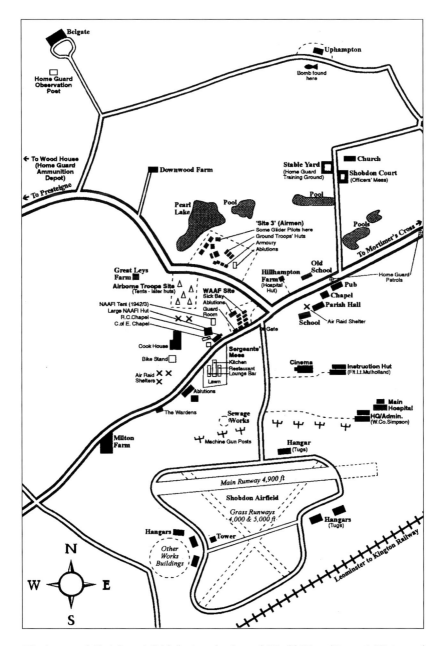

The layout of Shobdon airfield during the Second World War. (From A History of Shobdon by Ivor Pruell)

decided initially to locate the accommodation and messing facilities off-camp in the surrounding villages. From the beginning it was intended that the new airfield should have a hard runway together with two grass intersecting runways. A tarmac strip measuring 4,900 ft in length and 300 ft wide was laid together with the building of workshops, administrative buildings and instruction huts.

With construction continuing, the Fairey Battles and Westland Lysanders of No 8 Anti-aircraft Co-operation Unit arrived. Though just a small detachment, their duty was to work with the army and naval anti-aircraft units in the Midlands and Wales. Fine days would see them airborne allowing the gunners to fix their positions and learn how to work the range predictors for accurate firing. The unit later alternated between Shobdon and Madley for most of the war, finally being redesignated No 577 Squadron on 1 December 1943 and converting to Hurricanes and Oxfords.

The AACU aircraft were the only ones to be seen at Shobdon in those formative years. Its future use as a large training airfield came by coincidence when an RAF Avro Anson was forced to land at the airfield.

The daughter of Wg Cdr H.J. 'Tony' Davies, the pilot of the aircraft, takes up the story: 'My late father is attributed with the "founding" of Shobdon airfield. He joined the volunteer reserves aged 19 in December 1938 and learned to fly at Staverton airfield near Gloucester. By 1941 he was already instructing other trainee pilots. His family farmed near Ledbury and whenever he had the chance he would fly over and "buzz" them. It was on a training flight via Fishguard on 1 May 1942 that he had headed in that direction when the aircraft developed a fault which needed attention. His logbook (which is on long loan to the Imperial War Museum) states that he was flying an Anson with a crew of five and that he landed north of Leominster. My mother remembered the story that the aircraft was fixed and they took off again the next day from the flat fields where they had landed (Shobdon was little more than a cluster of houses, a tiny church and one or two farms in those days). When the air force heard that he had landed and taken off again from some fields, they realised it was a good place for an airfield. That became Shobdon. By the end of the war my father was a Wing Commander (aged 25) and master pilot of the elite Pathfinder force with a DSO, DFC and bar. He never, however, forgot that landing at Shobdon.'

Whilst the airmen and later the WAAFs were accommodated in the village until new huts were constructed, the officers' mess was at

Shobdon Court. Further buildings were requisitioned from local landowners as the personnel began to increase. A hint as to the future use of the airfield came when the tarmac runway was extended and widened. It was now nearly a mile long, one of the longest in either county. The construction of six T2 hangars together with Blister hangars also indicated that Shobdon was earmarked to become a major bomber base.

By the spring of 1942, with construction well advanced, it was decided that it would not be needed to support bombers. A signal was received stating that the airfield would become a base for training glider pilots. In early May, a party of five under the leadership of Flt Lt Skilling arrived to set up a temporary station headquarters. The arrival of Sqd Ldr Saward as acting CO of Shobdon saw No 5 Glider Training School transfer from Kidlington in Oxfordshire to Shobdon on 2 July 1942. By the end of the month, 230 personnel had arrived and several days later, the first two fuselages of Hotspur gliders were delivered for ground training.

First flown in November 1940, the General Aircraft Hotspur was produced to meet a specification calling for an assault glider able to

Glider pilots under training. (Imperial War Museum)

151

Hotspur MkII gliders airborne from Shobdon. (Imperial War Museum, CH6034)

glide 100 miles from its release point at 20,000 ft. It carried a pilot and had room for seven troops. By the time the war started it was basically considered too small for assault operations and so was relegated to a training role from the beginning. The initial production order for Hotspurs was 400 but in the end over 1,000 were built, mainly by Harris Lebus of Tottenham. It was the Mk II, the trainer version, that came to Shobdon, which had dual controls with the instructor and trainee sitting one behind the other, and was made entirely of wood and glue.

Encompassed within No 23 Group, the airfield became very busy as further Hotspurs were flown in from Kidlington. Only one incident marred an otherwise safe transfer when two Hotspurs collided on landing without injury to either pilot. Initially, a single Westland Lysander arrived for the purpose of air experience but was quickly supplemented by a variety of aircraft including the main monoplane RAF trainer, the Miles Magister, followed by the Miles Master. There were also a few Tiger Moths on strength for pilot familiarisation. By the end of the month, the CO was able to report that RAF Shobdon was operational.

A full flying programme began in August. At the same time, Sqd Ldr Saward relinquished his command of the station and handed over to Wg Cdr Matheson. Matheson stayed for the briefest of times before handing over to Sqd Ldr Gardiner who came to Shobdon from Weston-on-the-Green in Oxfordshire. As the training programme accelerated, so the accident record rose. As early as June 1942, PO Mason and Flt Sgt Shephard had perished in their Miles Master when it crashed into a field adjacent to the airfield. In another incident PO Chinery and Sgt Heidemann were killed when their Master crashed into a mountain near Llanwrtyd Wells. Though they were flying from Tern Hill and not Shobdon, it was Shobdon personnel that had the grim task of retrieving the bodies of the airmen.

Night flying now became part of the training programme and, with good weather, the diarist was able to record 446 glider flying hours by day and 57 by night. The training in powered flight had totalled 879 by day and 62 by night. Sqd Ldr Gardiner was pleased to report to Group a total of 1,721 flying hours since arrival. The rest of the year saw training continue, marred by the death of Sgt McLeer, a trainee, in a Hotspur which crashed onto the airfield. Although he was rushed to the Station Sick Quarters (SSQ), he later sadly died of his injuries. The pilot, Sgt Levison, suffered a dislocation of his left hip.

Christmas 1942 saw the opening of the station church. Since the arrival of the gliding school, regular worshippers had used the local village churches, both Anglican and Catholic. They were however some distance from the airfield and being small, could not accommodate the local people as well as the camp personnel. For some time the CO had made representation to the Group that Shobdon should have its own church and chaplain. When the Rev G.R. Cooper arrived from Cardington to take up the post of Chaplain, the choosing of a plot of land on the camp saw the construction of a concrete building to serve as an inter-denominational church. The first service was held over the Christmas period and four months later, a Roman Catholic chapel was built adjacent to the church.

The new year saw bad weather hampering the training programme. The usual routine for flying was that when coming in to land, the tug aircraft would use the hard runway whilst the gliders landed on the grass. With the heavy snow, all efforts had been concentrated on clearing the tarmac runway leaving the snow to melt naturally on the grass. When it did the area became a field of mud. The retrieval of the gliders was usually done by tractor. However, at this stage of the war Shobdon had just one or two and with the increased demand upon the school, it fell to engaging local farmers with their horses to assist in bringing the gliders back to the take-off point and the respective dispersals. With a small payment as an incentive, there was no shortage of offers!

As we have read, Shobdon was to have one of the longest and widest tarmac runways of the period. The unusual width would allow for the combination of glider and tug to land independently and be dispersed to one side whilst further traffic landed alongside. The two grass runways were Runway 14/32, being 4,100 ft in length, and 04/22 at 5,170 ft, both 150 ft wide.

Bad weather during January and February hampered pilot training and may have been a factor in an incident that happened on 6th February. Although snow still lay on the grass, the tarmac runway had been cleared and it was decided to attempt a full day's flying training. One of the groundcrew on duty, Cpl Devenport, was allocated the job of wingman which entailed holding one of the glider's wings clear of the ground until the moment the tug aircraft began to pull the glider. Unfortunately on one particular launch, Cpl Devenport was struck by the wing of the glider as it gathered speed and was killed. A similar accident happened to Sgt A.G. Dixon, also a member of the groundcrew, who was killed when he was struck by a glider whilst manning the flare path during a night exercise.

With improving weather and longer days, the training programme was accelerated. A change from routine came in March 1943 when a detachment of Douglas Boston 111a's arrived. Part of No 88 (Hong Kong) Squadron, then operating from the large grass airfield of Swanton Morley in Norfolk, they were based at Shobdon for smoke laying trials connected to the planned invasion. First shipped to the UK in 1941, the Boston was modified for use with No 2 Group on anti-shipping strikes and small scale daylight bombing raids on the Continent. As the invasion approached they were used in trials of different smoke effects for use over the beaches in order to screen the landing troops. For a year there were times when Shobdon was enveloped in smoke but the trials were to prove their worth when the landings began.

March also saw the opening of a new entertainments hall in North Road. This was to serve as a cinema, dance hall and concert hall and was to be used on many occasions by ENSA. Having been starved of entertainment since the airfield opened, its opening was welcomed by all the station personnel.

Over the night of 15/16 September 1943 a formation of 369 aircraft was detailed to carry out a moonlit raid on the Dunlop rubber factory at Montlucon in Central France. With the Pathfinders marking the target accurately and the Master Bomber following on behind to drop its bombs directly on the target, it was a devastating raid.

Taking part in the bombing were five American B-17s. Once the bombs had been dropped, all five turned for home. It was a very cloudy return and one of the B-17s, short of fuel and with its navigational systems knocked out, flew low over Herefordshire with a terrified crew looking desperately for a hole in the cloud in the hope of seeing a flat area of land in which to put the aircraft down. For ten long hours they had been in the air and now, the large runway at Shobdon lit by a burst of moonlight gave them hope. Putting the aircraft into a steep dive, they came out of the cloud as Shobdon loomed up before them. They were saved from a horrible death by the 'long runway in the middle of nowhere', as the pilot called it. One month later a Thunderbolt pilot also had cause to thank Shobdon when, returning from a mission over France low on fuel and shot up, he saw the big runway and landed safely.

Day after day the skies above Shobdon were filled with gliders and their tug aircraft. With plans for D-Day at an advanced stage, the airfield was becoming increasingly busy. Douglas Smithson was one of the men in training for the big day. Previously a Sapper in No 246 Field

A familiar scene at Shobdon, though in this case the gliders are being towed by Hawker Hectors. (RAF Museum)

Company, Royal Engineers, the change to glider pilot was very welcome, as he recalls:

'Rescued from Dunkirk, we landed at Ramsgate on Saturday, 1 June 1940. My diary says a red letter day because we had made it back. Our entry to the port was wonderful. I was wet to the skin after the hole I had to swim out of and had lost my kit except for my small pack. We were welcomed by the local people and taken by bus to the nearby railway station. A special train then took us to Tidworth Camp where we slept and ate under canvas. One morning I was laying on my back outside the tent and at the same time I was looking up at a plane flying overhead. I knew it to be a Short Stirling but little did I think then that later in the war I should fly a Horsa glider behind one.

'Over the following years I was posted to many places in the UK but from my diary I see that in the autumn of 1942 I was posted to Wallingford. Being very fed up with appearing not to be doing much to hasten the end of the war, I see also that at this time I applied to join the Glider Pilot Regiment which had not been formed long. It clearly

Trainee glider pilots take a NAAFI break at Shobdon – the glider is a Hotspur. (Crown via Air Britain)

did not get through as I never heard anything else about my application. So I continued to be posted around the UK lecturing to new recruits etc until I see that 27 September 1943 was a very important day in my life. Off duty in the evening, I was in a canteen and saw, on a notice board, a request asking for glider pilots and that no person should be stopped applying unless they were scheduled for abroad. I once again diligently applied, requesting a transfer to the Army Air Corps for training as a glider pilot. A short time elapsed before I was called to an interview in Edinburgh. There I had to sit a maths paper as well as an intelligence one. More papers to fill in and then an aptitude test on a makeshift cockpit. I then had an interview before a selection board before returning to my unit and awaiting my fate. By 8 December 1943 I had been told that my application had been successful and packed up my belongings and caught a train to Salisbury Plain. I had finished my career as a Sapper and was looking forward to whatever the next few years held for me.

'I spent about ten days on Salisbury Plain before heading for the airfield at Booker to join an Elementary Flying Training School. Over the last few days of 1943 I had my first flight in an aeroplane, a Tiger Moth. The instructor took off and got me acclimatised and then let me take over. Quite different to what I had imagined. One had to use so little effort to move the control stick, you just eased it from one position to the direction required. The same action was needed by the feet on the rudder pedals. After a few days, flying in the air was not too difficult. Taking off also became easier after some trial attempts and confidence given by the instructor. Landing was not easy as control of the speed and height of the Tiger at the same time required effort and practice. Once one got the idea of judging the height from the horizon and the ability to feel the plane on to the ground, things got more enjoyable and flying became the fun that one always thought it would be. Finally came the big day, entirely without warning. I was surprised when the Chief Flying Instructor came and said that he was taking me up for my eight hour test. I took off and did all the flying myself. On touching down he got out and told me to stay in and take her for a circuit and landing on my own. No time for any doubts. I was in the air before I had time to think and in no time at all I was rolling in to land. I had made my first solo. I was then brought down to earth as the instructor, after congratulating me, told me I could now start learning to fly!

'It now became almost daily routine to fly circuits and bumps, gradually attempting more difficult manoeuvres. After about ten hours, I had my first night flight. At first this was very strange as everything was so different but again after a number of flights one got used to it. On reaching eleven hours and foolishly beginning to think I could fly, I learnt that one could have too much confidence. I was told to do a few solo circuits and bumps and so I started off into the air with ease, never lost sight of the airfield and came into land. At the last minute another Tiger took off in front of me and as instructed I pushed the throttle forward and went round for a second circuit and came round to land again. This time I bounced and had to rise again to do another circuit. Now I was not too happy! Third time trying to land I bumped too much again and so round once more. I was now beginning to think that I was going to stay in the air forever. This time all was well and I made a good landing. Even so my confidence was shaken and it took a few days to get back the feeling that I might be able to fly properly some day.'

The initial flying instruction completed, Douglas was now ready to move on to Shobdon: 'We were obviously wanted in the regiment because when we had finished 16 hours' flying and had made our first solo flight, we were moved to Shobdon. Here we began our first glider training. I had an acclimatisation flight in a Hotspur and from the first I enjoyed flying it. It could carry about ten men and when I flew it

An army corporal climbs into the cockpit of a Hotspur glider. (Imperial War Museum)

there was only the instructor and myself. The instructor sat in the back seat and to begin with we did a few circuits and bumps and then more adventurous things. The first time I stalled in the Hotspur it was quite frightening, much more than in the Tiger. I followed the instructor's orders and raised the nose until we had very little airspeed. I thought we were going up forever when suddenly the end of the world occurred, at least it seemed like it! I watched the ASI [airspeed indicator] and somewhere around 35 AS, we dropped out of the sky. I pushed the stick forward and then eased back and we slowly flattened out and I breathed more easily. Next was to solo. After this I started to enjoy most of the flying that we did. In free flight, after I had pulled off from the tug, a Miles Master, it was almost like riding a motor cycle. Near the village of Shobdon was a wood and when flying over it, with care, one could almost hover. The currents of air were so strong that the glider almost stopped and only slowly eased downwards with a kind of rocking motion.'

Once having mastered the Hotspur in daylight, Douglas then had to do the same at night: 'Night flying was a different kettle of fish. My first order from the instructor was that on touchdown I was to give it full left rudder. My first circuit and I tentatively pushed my left foot forward on touching down whereupon the glider went slightly left. This did not please him and whilst waiting for the tractor to pull us back to the start, he told me again to give it more left rudder. The third time he was starting to get annoyed and said he did not want to be on the airfield all night! Therefore the next circuit as soon as we touched the ground I really stood on the left rudder bar. We swung almost at right angles and careered sideways down the airfield. I expected the wing to drop at any time and crumple but it didn't. The undercarriage shook but remarkably no tyres burst and we came to a stop. The instructor complimented me and we were soon ready to continue. I did the same for the remaining circuits and we had a fairly early night! At Shobdon I flew another powered aircraft for the first time. It was a Miles Magister. In this plane I was instructed in elementary navigation. After a sortie around the Brecon Beacons, he told me to take over and fly us back to the airfield. I did and after landing he complimented me on returning directly on a reciprocal bearing. I did not enlighten him on that; I had only a slight knowledge of what a reciprocal was. I had seen the railway line just after having taken over and as it ran alongside the airfield there was not much difficulty in finding the way back.'

As the run-up to D-Day continued, the heavy usage of the grass runway caused it to become very rutted and dangerous to landing aircraft. In order to alleviate this problem, Sommerfeld Track was laid to allow all-weather serviceability. Around the same time the civilian tractors were replaced by brightly coloured yellow Jeeps as Mr C.K. Slade, a flying instructor, recalled in a letter to the *Hereford Times* in 1990:

'In September 1944 I was a flying instructor at No 26 EFTS at Booker airfield but when the Glider Regiment was lost at Arnhem that same month, I was posted to Shobdon. There, after a short conversion course, I instructed glider pilots for further operations in Europe, notably the Rhine crossing. I was at Shobdon from early October to late March 1945. Regarding the width of the runway, I am inclined to doubt if the wide runway was just for the convenience of glider pilots landing, certainly no glider pilot was allowed to land on it during my time. The runway, or "towline" as it was then known, was an extremely busy place. At the down-wind end there would be a queue of gliders and these would be towed into the air in succession, just as quickly as the ground staff could attach the tow ropes. When the glider

The cargo for Shobdon-trained glider pilots – paratroopers prepare around D-Day.
(SE Newspapers)

reached the required height for whatever exercise the pilot intended to carry out, he would release his end of the rope and eventually land on the large grass area to the south of the runway. Meanwhile the tugs would be flying with a long tow rope ending in a steel hook, dangling below. The pilot would release this into the dropping zone on the north side of the airfield, then land on the unoccupied half of the runway and start all over again with the yellow Jeeps collecting the tow ropes for the next sortie.'

Being a training school, it was not only the gliders that sometimes came to grief. The tug aircraft were often flown by trainee pilots, which resulted in several fatal accidents, as Douglas Smithson recalls once again.

'There was one sad affair during my stay at Shobdon. I was again on night flying and it was on our second circuit when the instructor noticed that the combination that had taken off in front of us was losing height. I took more notice of it and realised that the Magister was not climbing as it should have been doing. The glider pilot had noticed it as well and had pulled off. As he did so the Magister plunged to the ground and soon burst into flames. The glider landed easily close by helped by the light from the burning Magister. At the time we thought that no-one had been killed but only injured. Much later I heard that the pilot and his trainee were both killed.

'Before I leave Shobdon I must record another happening. I had been put on ground duty as extra ground staff and was armed with an Aldis lamp, in this case with a red light only, and I had to use it to point at anything that needed a warning. I thought I should have nothing to do except watch gliders and tugs take off and land. I was sadly mistaken.

'After about an hour or so I saw coming in from the other end of the railway line, a Magister obviously preparing to land. It was about half a mile away and I became interested to see what kind of landing he was going to make. The pilot seemed to be doing everything correctly and I thought he must be well experienced. Looking a little harder I noticed that his undercarriage was not down. I pointed the lamp at the Magister and kept it on the cockpit as well as I could but the plane continued flying past me at 30 ft and as it passed I could hear the warning buzzer going, something was wrong. He touched down about 30 yds from me and made a beautiful belly landing. The pilot jumped out quickly in case of fire and all was well. The underwings were torn off along with part of the fuselage. The prop was obviously bent but the damage looked repairable. Talking with the pilot before he reported to flying control, he explained that he had seen my red

The Horsa was the main assault glider of the war. (Imperial War Museum, CH10366)

light on him but there was little he could do. His undercarriage had jammed some time before when he had tried to land. Ground control had told him to fly around again and get rid of most of his fuel and then come in again. He did just that and because of the lack of fuel, the aircraft did not catch fire. Despite the incidents, I hold fond memories of my time at Shobdon.'

Douglas was to take part in Operation Overlord and flew a Horsa glider towed by a Short Stirling in the first waves to go in. Landing his aircraft and troops safely somewhere in the region of the River Orne, he wished them good luck before making his way back to Dunkirk where a ship collected him and other pilots before landing them back at Newhaven. He took part in the Arnhem operation on 18 September 1944 where again he flew a Horsa glider. Unfortunately the tow rope gave way as they were over the Channel and Douglas had to decide to either ditch the glider close to the shore or try to glide to *terra firma*. With his co-pilot he decided to make for land and came down for a

A painting by Keith Woodcock depicting a Stirling IV, showing the towing yoke under the gun turret. (K. Woodcock)

perfect landing. Unfortunately the area was held by the Germans and Douglas became a POW for the rest of the war.

Back at Shobdon, training for the invasion continued. With part of the runway undergoing resurfacing, the Glider Instructor Flight was detached to a relief landing ground at Hockley Heath near Solihull in Warwickshire. This was to be given full satellite status to Shobdon in May 1944. On the eve of the invasion, both airfields, like the rest in the region, were shut down for 48 hours. With the losses of gliders and crews over the invasion period, the schedule was accelerated to train pilots for the forthcoming Operation Market Garden, the Arnhem landings.

Often called the greatest of airborne operations, the invasion of Holland on 17 September 1944 followed by the advance of the British 2nd Army to the lower reaches of the Rhine, was daring and imaginative. The American landings took place as planned and the troops soon reached their bridges. The RAF, concerned about the air defence at Arnhem, had a dropping zone well away from the town. Consequently troops had a long march to their objective and met fierce enemy resistance along the way. Of the paratroopers that did reach Arnhem, many fought and died and after a very intense combat, the remainder were forced to surrender. Eindhoven, Grave, Nijmegen and Arnhem became familiar names to many glider pilots trained at Shobdon. Unfortunately the Glider Regiment suffered badly in this operation, losing 615 pilots; 90 per cent of the Regiment was used in 'Market Garden', a total of 1,126 men. Although the landings were achieved successfully and the British troops won the admiration of the world, it was at a tremendous cost.

With further airborne assaults in the planning, the training programme at Shobdon was pushed to its limit. Life had suddenly changed with work continuing from eight in the morning until well into the night. Leave, unless essential, was cancelled and many meals were taken at the place of work. Such was the shortage of glider pilots that many were conscripted from RAF powered flight aircrew to learn to fly gliders. They were not volunteers, they were told to move to Shobdon and although they did not have to join the Regiment, they were forced to wear khaki battledress whilst retaining their blue berets (a formality that continues to this day with the Army Air Corps). The WAAFs were also subjected to more rigorous hours, repairing the fabric covering of the gliders, radios, tow ropes etc. Many WAAF ex-barrage balloon operators were sent to Shobdon for there were few enemy aircraft over the country at this late period of the war and with fewer balloons needed, their knowledge was put to use as fabric repairers and flight mechanics.

The intense training brought the inevitable spate of crashes including both Master tugs and gliders. Wg Cdr Simpson, who had arrived to command Shobdon in May 1943, was to see the school through its most demanding period. A strict disciplinarian, he believed that despite the pressures, correct dress was to be worn at all times and that health and hygiene together with fitness should be paramount. He also arranged several talks to be given by officers from Brize Norton who had experienced the Normandy operations at first hand. After so many losses of glider pilots in the recent airborne operations, he felt that this would boost morale. What did boost morale was the fact that everyone hoped that Christmas 1944 would be the last one of the war. The usual customs were observed at Shobdon on the 25th with the officers serving the other ranks lunch before retiring to their own mess. During the dinner Wg Cdr Simpson reminded his audience that until the war had actually ended, there would be no let-up on the rigorous training schedule.

By January 1945, personnel numbers at Shobdon had risen to 1,127. This was to remain constant until May when, with victory in Europe, some relaxation of training took place. VE Day was celebrated on 8th May with a service of thanksgiving held in the station cinema, the Astra. It was then a day of celebration for all ranks. Several days later large parades and demonstrations of glider techniques were held to which the general public were invited, eager to see at first hand what role Shobdon had played in the defeat of Nazi Germany; VJ Day on 15th August saw a similar display for the public. With a final parade being held on the 18 October 1945, the diarist recorded: 'No 5 Glider Training School disbanded today.'

It fell to Wg Cdr Mullen to close the station down as it went into Care and Maintenance. The military had no further use for gliders and many of the Hotspurs at Shobdon were either flown into storage elsewhere or broken up as the airfield became a detached site of No 25 MU. No further use was to be made of the site and many buildings began to fall into decay. It remained this way until the Herefordshire Aero Club, looking for a new home, visited Shobdon and found it suited their purposes admirably. In 1961 they established the Aero Club there and it is their premises that we find at Shobdon today. Operated by Shobdon Sports and Leisure Ltd, part of the huge asphalt runway, 09/27 (900 yds x 18 yds), remains and is used by aircraft both visiting and belonging to the club.

Wartime buildings at Shobdon are now used by the Herefordshire Aero Club. (Author)

One of the old wartime T2 hangars is still in use for club aircraft but sadly the 518/40 control tower has been pulled down. Shobdon is sometimes difficult to find, hidden as it is in low-lying country surrounded by trees, and a Non-Directional Beacon was installed in 1970 to aid the many private airmen using the airfield today. Never again will lumbering Hotspur gliders be seen in the area. Never again will men like Douglas Smithson lift off from its huge runway to take an engineless aeroplane to war. All the hard work and training had paid dividends and Shobdon had played its part in the final victory.

9
WORCESTER (PERDISWELL)

As with many towns and cities in the British Isles, it was the National Aviation Display Tours of Alan Cobham that first brought flying to the attention of the people of Worcester. It is recorded that his 'Flying Circus' came to Worcester, presumably Pitchcroft airfield as it then was, on 19 June 1934. The previous years had seen flying demonstrations by Colonel Samuel Franklin Cody and the German, Gustav Hamel, but it was Cobham who gave local people the chance to experience flight. And all of this at the cost of one shilling.

The military and aviation roots of the city, however, lie during the First World War when the Royal Engineers established the first military wireless unit at nearby Norton Barracks. From the area known as Pitchcroft, now the Worcester horse racing track, they flew large kites fitted with trailing aerials in order to experiment in communications. With the ending of the conflict in 1918 the site reverted to civilian use, as Max Sinclair of Worcester recalls:

'Pitchcroft was a natural arena for the early balloonists and aviators to display their skill, or lack of it, to adoring crowds. An early monoplane flight in 1910 ended in tragedy when the plane slewed into the crowd. This killed a lady near my mother, who told me "her hatpin was driven through her head". No doubt she had a fractured skull as well but that wasn't so dramatic. Cody returned during the 1930s but by now Pitchcroft was in the centre of an ever growing city and on common land which could not be closed to the public so the council established a safer flying field on a large estate at Perdiswell Hall, to the north of the city. When this new site opened it was reputed to be the first real municipal airfield in the world.

'When Cody's Circus arrived the non-paying public had their view restricted by lining the airfield with six-foot high hessian barriers.

Balloon experiments such as these were carried out by the Royal Engineers at Pitchcroft. (D. Collyer)

Small boys (such as me) found if they pushed a pencil between the threads, an eye hole could be created through which to watch the smoking dogfights. This was until the local policeman found us and clipped a few ears. Going back to Pitchcroft, in 1928 a Lieutenant Paul made a landing there. Sadly, on take-off he experienced engine power loss, made the mistake of trying to turn back, stalled and crashed with fatal results. His subsequent funeral at the Cathedral was attended by thousands of citizens, even to the extent of lining the roads.'

When Pitchcroft closed, as Max Sinclair indicated, it forced the council to look elsewhere for a suitable site for a municipal aerodrome. Several were looked at including Battenhall, Powick-Ham and Norton. Eventually it chose an area two miles north of the centre of Worcester, lying alongside the Worcester and Birmingham Canal, called Perdiswell.

Before putting its proposals for the new airfield before the Ministry of Aviation, the council was told that in selecting a site it must take into consideration the following factors: the soil should be medium to light in weight; the land should be level and on a plateau; ridges and furrows should be avoided; the ideal aerodrome should be close to the heart of the city which it serves; the site should afford at least 800 yds run into any wind; it should be free from fog and pollution.

The council agreed that it could meet almost all the criteria and the decision was taken to go ahead. The price set was £6,500 and the land was duly purchased. However, before work on the new airfield could begin, further land had to be acquired. In 1935 compulsory requisition orders were handed to the owners of Astwood Farm and Spring Bank Farm together with another notice to Cadbury's who also owned some of the land. After a period of intensive levelling and removing of obstacles, the council called upon the En Tout Cas Company to plant new grass seed.

Over the next few years it promoted the airport throughout the country, calling it Worcester Municipal Airport, a name that it hoped would induce aviation companies and aircraft to use the new site. That it was proving attractive to some companies is shown by a letter dated 25 April 1936 from Mr Whitney-Straight, a well known aviator of the time, stating that he would like to take over the running of the new Worcester Airport. He pointed out that he already ran municipal airports at Ramsgate, Plymouth, Ipswich and Exeter. An exchange of letters went on for some considerable time between the two parties but nothing was to come of it. This was the first of several setbacks for the council.

Not downhearted however, it entered into correspondence with the General Aircraft Company which was based at Feltham near London and which had expressed an interest in leasing the airport for its own use. It even offered to set up a unit of the Civil Air Guard to train civilians to fly in addition to the military flying schools. However, with one unit of the CAG already being run by Worcestershire Flying Club at nearby Throckmorton airfield, later to become RAF Pershore, it was felt there was no need for a second in the same area. Negotiations continued with General Aircraft for some time without a firm resolution. So much time passed by that the MP for Worcester, the Hon W. Lindsay-Everard, wrote to Mr C.H. Digby-Seymour, the town clerk, asking whether General Aircraft were going to exercise their option to use Perdiswell. In the end it did not and with the signs of another war approaching, the council offered the airfield to the Air Ministry.

Although small, with the rapid expansion of the military fields Perdiswell seemed to fit the criteria very well. With all the necessary legal requirements satisfied, the site was renamed RAF Perdiswell, also known as Worcester. The nearby Perdiswell Hall, a Victorian

The all-grass airfield at Perdiswell, 1944. (Dennis Williams)

mansion of some considerable size, was also requisitioned and became the headquarters of No 81 Group, Fighter Command.

Even though the weather over the winter of 1937/8 was wet and cold with frequent snowfalls, completion came by 1938 with the first aircraft to arrive being several Fairey Battles. The Battle was one of the key types chosen by the Air Ministry to equip the rapidly expanding air force. It was a gigantic step up from the biplane bombers in that it could carry twice as many bombs twice as far. It was also the first monoplane bomber to enter service. However, in the event it proved under-powered with its one Rolls-Royce Merlin 1 engine, as well as being under-armed with its single Browning machine gun forward and one Vickers 'K' gun aft. It was obsolescent before it came into service but, with Bomber Command needing a modern looking aircraft with which to attack the enemy, it remained in service until as late as September 1940.

The aircraft that flew into Worcester on that squally, rainy day in 1938 had been built at the Austin Motor Works at Longbridge near Birmingham. Although the type was initially built by Fairey Aviation at Stockbridge, the Austin-built Battles came under the umbrella of the Shadow Factory Scheme. Their arrival at Worcester heralded the start

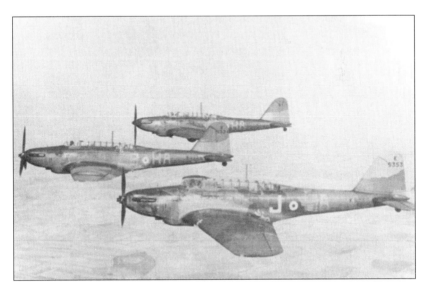

Fairey Battle bombers of No 218 Squadron. This type was test-flown to Worcester (Perdiswell). (Air Britain)

of operations from the airfield although the Battles had arrived purely for flight testing before being passed on to operational squadrons, painted with circles of alternate yellow and black for identification purposes. It was said at the time that if they reached Worcester from Longbridge, a few miles away, they had passed their test! For almost four years the Fairey Battles were to use Worcester for pre-delivery testing. The last aircraft to leave the Austin production line was a trainer (V1280) delivered on 2 September 1940. The final 235 aircraft were cancelled. Its one moment of glory came on 20 September 1940 when a Battle rear gunner claimed the first German aircraft shot down during the war in the west. That same month the type was relegated to training duties.

The Battle of Britain had very little effect on Worcester although from time to time enemy aircraft were heard within the area. Most of this was at night and the Air Ministry, in their wisdom, detached a single Boulton Paul Defiant to 'act in the role of a night-fighter'.

One of the airmen to witness its arrival was Alex Hunter: 'I remember the arrival of the Defiant. It was painted black all over and was to be used in the event of enemy aircraft attacking Worcester at night and for the defence of the Black Country. How on earth it was thought it would ever find an aircraft in the dark confounded me. I don't think it could have got off at night as there was no real runway lighting. When on the odd occasion there was flying after dark, we had to put goose-neck flares alongside the runway and be ready to put them out if an enemy aircraft came along. The Defiant had a very early radar of some sort. It was quite a hard life for us airmen at Worcester. We had to dig slit trenches and were doing training under instruction from the Worcestershire Regiment. I remember the Battle bombers that were being tested at the airfield looked like wasps with their yellow and black stripes. Worcester was a pleasant posting and really was not at all warlike.'

The airfield, although not attacked by the Luftwaffe, did see several accidents. One of the first to happen was on 24 May 1940 when a Bristol Blenheim of No 53 Squadron was approaching Worcester to collect some spark plugs from the maintenance section. Being a small airfield, the pilot went round twice to gauge his approach. Attempting one landing, he realised he could not make the runway and applying full power, gained some height and went round again. The next time, coming in low over the boundary, his wheels touched the grass and though settling down to continue his run, the aircraft ran out of landing area. Despite fully applying his brakes, the pilot could not stop the Blenheim and it overshot the end of the airfield boundary, crashing through some iron railings and onto a road. Sitting on the railings at this time was 16-year-old Beryl Smith of Southfield Street in Worcester. The aircraft careered onto the Bilford Road, sadly killing Beryl and injuring four others when it hit a car.

Barely one month later another Blenheim suffered failure of the port engine on its approach. Attempting to gain height in order to complete another circuit, the aircraft crashed, killing the pilot, Sgt T.L. Armstrong. The size of the landing ground also accounted for another crash, this time of an aircraft of the USAAF.

The morning of 2 September 1942 was cloudy with squally showers. At around 10.00 hrs a C-47 Dakota named *Idiot's Delight* suffered an engine failure just after take-off from Pershore and looked for a place to land. The pilot saw Worcester and commenced a landing run. Owing to the wet grass, once again an overshoot took place and the aircraft finished up through the railings and onto the Bilford Road, again blocking it completely. The aircraft was supposedly carrying General Carl 'Tooey' Spaatz, Commanding General of the USAAF in England.

Once again, Max Sinclair was in the right place at the right time: 'The incident which has been the greatest mystery was in September 1942 when a Dakota named *"Idiot's Delight"* was forced to land at Worcester. On board was an American film crew planning a gunnery training film for the newly arrived American Army Air Force based on RAF experience. In the aircraft was General Spaatz who, after the aircraft had slid across Bilford Road into the City Corporation rubbish tip, commented, "I didn't cross the Atlantic to land in the town trash pile!" In the co-pilot's seat was the film star Clark Gable who had hitched a lift with the film crew to experience some action. When the accident happened, people helped the General out, as he had a broken ankle, before they all went off to Perdiswell Hall for something strong to drink. I remember FO Davis, who was lodging with us, coming home that night and telling my mother who he had been entertaining. My mother pretended to swoon, the first time I had experienced such a thing. Bilford Road was blocked for some time until the plane was dismantled. The Americans gave away large bars of chocolate and one of the Tiger Moth pilots tied a streamer on one to drop in my garden. Unfortunately it went through the roof tiles at another house and father was not best pleased.'

Several days later a Wellington Ic (DV 937) of No 16 OTU took off from Upper Heyford in Oxfordshire at 11.00 hrs for a routine cross

One of the only known photographs of the Dakota Idiot's Delight *that overshot at Worcester airfield. (Max Sinclair)*

country flight, piloted by Sgt K.J. Johnson of the RNZAF. Forty-five minutes into the flight the port engine failed. Realising that they were near Worcester airfield, the pilot warned the crew that he was going to attempt a landing. Retracting his undercarriage, he came in over the boundary and dropped the Wellington onto the grass. With a lot of wrenching and squealing, the aircraft slid along the grass, passed through the boundary fence and came to a rest in the corner of the airfield. Though the aircraft was badly damaged, all five crewmen survived.

As well as Bilford Road the large lake at Perdiswell Hall claimed a victim. One of the more notable crashes into the lake was of a Whitley bomber that had been shot up during a raid somewhere over Europe.

This time Alex Hunter was in the right place at the wrong time: 'I was posted to Worcester in June 1941 and I remember many of the plane crashes. One bad one was when a Whitley crash-landed on the grass airfield and carried on going. I was in a gun pit at the end of the landing area which was really just a hole in the ground. I was manning the Lewis gun when the aircraft passed over me, taking the Lewis gun with it as it slithered down into the lake. This caused my gun to fire automatically and bullets were flying everywhere. When it stopped and I had recovered from the shock, I rushed down to the aircraft which was smoking heavily as the crew struggled to get out. I grabbed the air gunner and helped him up the slope when more of my comrades arrived. We eventually got them to the sick quarters where they were checked over before leaving a day later for Pershore to fight another day.'

A new unit arrived at Worcester on 18th April in the form of No 2 Elementary Flying School (EFTS). Previously stationed at Staverton in Gloucestershire the unit flew the venerable Tiger Moth. Using Perdiswell Hall as their headquarters, Wg Cdr T.W. Campbell, AFC, arrived to command the unit at the same time. Almost immediately the weather interrupted the flying schedule as the Official Record Book recorded: '31st August – The weather for the month was poor for the season. 22 half days were unfit for flying.'

The Tiger Moth, used for flying training with No 2 EFTS at Worcester. (Aeroplane)

179

Personnel of No 2 EFTS in front of Perdiswell Hall, 1940. (Roy Gilmour)

The weather was also to be responsible for several accidents, one of which happened on 20 March 1943, a generally overcast day. A thick haze had prevented any flying until noon. At around 13.00 hrs with a gradual improvement forecast, Sgt Barber, an Australian pilot, and Sgt Dunn, a Canadian trainee, got aboard Tiger Moth R5203 for a pinpointing and map reading exercise. Taking off, they were around 15 minutes into the flight when the aircraft suddenly dived into the ground from around 600 ft and caught fire. Sadly both men were burnt to death.

Once again Max Sinclair takes up the story: 'a flying school was started teaching raw RAF pilots on a Link Trainer and then Tiger Moths. The senior instructor was FO Davis who with his family was billeted at my home in Ombersley Road. Perdiswell, as we called it, was known as a "Lavatory Emergency Airfield" and from time to time larger aircraft, some shot up, arrived spectacularly to slide onto the road or slip into the lake alongside Perdiswell Hall. Wellingtons, Hampdens, Ansons and Whitleys, they all suffered the same fate, sometimes with tragic results. One particular aircraft, a de Havilland Dove, flew around on a test before a planned flight for some of us locals. Unfortunately its brakes failed and it went through the hedge by Cadbury's factory. I managed to acquire a large perspex window as a souvenir before, as was the case with all the crashes, the aircraft was loaded onto a "Queen Mary" trailer and taken away. There were many escapades with novice pilots; one flew under Upton on Severn bridge and left a bit of his wing as incriminating evidence.

'However, what could have been a tragedy turned into a light hearted incident just before Christmas 1943. A young Tiger Moth pilot was sent on a cross-country flight over Shropshire. After some hours there was no sign of him or any message so another aircraft with an instructor and crewman was sent to follow the planned route. Again, nothing was heard from them and we received a telephone message at our house for FO Davis to report to Worcester urgently. He set off in a third plane and somewhere out in the wilds he spotted the other two aircraft parked on the immaculate lawn of a large country house. Apparently the first Tiger Moth had run out of fuel and had landed on the first clear area of grass that he had seen. The second one, upon seeing the aircraft parked on the lawn, had landed to offer assistance to the first. Both crews had been received by a large private party of pretty girls who welcomed the brave young men. When FO Davis and his crewman landed, they too were welcomed with open arms which led to a party and rather a lot of drink. A message eventually reached

The remaining Maycrete hut at Worcester (Perdiswell). (Author)

Worcester that it was too late to refuel the first errant plane and a return was planned for the next day. I remember covering my ears when I heard FO Davis' wife welcome him home!'

The EFTS supported two flights, A and B with six to eight Tiger Moths to each flight. Whilst the flying was strictly military, the maintenance of the aircraft and the upkeep of the airfield was in the hands of civilians employed by the Bristol Aeroplane Company. The airfield was very basic with no navigational aids whatsoever and, the Tiger Moth having an open cockpit, the instructors and trainees would wrap up in layers of clothing topped up with sheepskin jackets. Most of the personnel lived off camp and lodged with the local people.

A relief landing ground was provided at Littleworth and, although only used on the odd occasion, did see tragedy when a Miles Master II crashed on 22 May 1943. The little aircraft was being ferried from Hullavington to Tern Hill airfield by a ferry pilot of the Air Transport Auxiliary, Second Officer Mary Nicholson, an American serving with the unit at Cosford. She had been a pre-war pilot of exceptional skill

Trainee pilots and a Tiger Moth at Worcester. (Roy Gilmour)

during the barnstorming days of aviation with displays of wing walking and other dangerous stunts. Sadly her life ended far from home when the Master crashed due to apparent lack of oil causing the engine to seize in flight.

It was incidents such as these that brought the war to RAF Worcester. The training continued right up until the end of the war. As D-Day approached, a signal was received stating that the airfield should be prepared to receive a number of wounded British and American troops once the invasion had begun. The area around Worcester had many American hospitals to which the wounded would be taken and treated. With the landings on the coast of Normandy, there began a regular service for the wounded flown into the airfield by Argus and Anson aircraft.

The end of the war saw no further use for Worcester and flying ceased in 1945. The city council gained the airfield back from the military and retained it for a recreational area. Over the years housing has gradually encroached upon this area, so that much of the green site has disappeared. Though it was never a major airfield, many aircrew did their initial training from Worcester.

10
THE MINOR
AIRFIELDS

Many of the small private airfields and strips that had been closed on the outbreak of the Second World War would never open again after it, including, in Herefordshire, Michaelchurch airfield. The old racecourse at Llandrindod Wells was another, as was the King's Acre Road site, used pre-war for civilian flying.

However, some people had a vision of light aviation returning to the area. At Holmer Road Racecourse, for instance, negotiations began after the war with Hereford City Council which soon included the Ministry of Civil Aviation. In August 1947 two grass runways were completed in the middle of the racecourse with a licence being issued by the Ministry on 9 August 1947. Aircraft (Hereford) was in business. It changed its name to Inter-City Air Services Ltd in 1948 but after relations soured with the council and the ministry, the licence was withdrawn on 10 May 1951.

Berrow

Sometimes known as Pendock Moor, Berrow was situated six miles west of Tewkesbury. Opened in March 1941 as a grass satellite landing ground, it saw very limited use and was handed over to No 38 Maintenance Unit in August 1942. The surface was found to be too uneven for use by many aircraft but was suitable for gliders and their

Only the water tower remains at the Comberton GCI station close to Pershore airfield. (Author)

tugs and, from September 1942, No 5 Glider Training School (GTS) based at Shobdon carried out practice glider landings at the site. It seemed perfect for this purpose but when it was found out that No 23 Group, in which No 5 GTS was encompassed, had no authority to use the airfield, all flying ceased. The Telecommunications Flying Unit (TFU) from Defford did use the limited facilities for a time but what looked to be a promising airfield for wartime operations was used very little. It closed in May 1945 and the land was returned to agriculture.

Comberton

Comberton was a self-contained Ground Controlled Interception (GCI) station consisting of operational and maintenance blocks. The radar masts were some distance away from the site whilst the living quarters were at Pershore. Now an industrial site, the one remaining link with the past is the water tower.

Boughrood Court

A 25 acre field here was requisitioned by the Air Ministry for use as an Emergency Landing Ground (ELG), but never used.

Chepstow Racecourse

The racecourse was taken over by the Air Ministry in May 1941 and became known as No 7 Satellite Landing Ground. Many Spitfires were held in reserve on the site but it was returned to its civilian owners in March 1945.

Lower Lugg Meadows

A site used for Air Cadet Gliding training up to 1946, when it was closed down.

Somerfield tracking taken from a Herefordshire airfield provides excellent farm gates.

11
AIRCRAFT AND
MUNITIONS FACTORIES

Rotherwas

At the end of the First World War most of the munitions factories closed. It was felt that no more would man go to war with man as the world looked forward to a brighter future. With several sites being mothballed for alternative uses, only one remained fully open, that being Woolwich Arsenal. Some sceptics, however, felt that another war was possible and that the Arsenal was vulnerable to air attack being so close to London. Thoughts turned to another munitions factory situated in the heart of Herefordshire and far from the battle front. Its name was Rotherwas.

Originally a 2,577 acre country estate dominated by a large manor house, Rotherwas dated from the 1450s when it belonged to the de la Barre family. Later years saw it purchased by many noble families until 1907 when the house was badly damaged by fire. Five years later the house and estate were auctioned with the County Council purchasing 195 acres of land and the rest, including the house, being sold to a Hereford businessman.

When, following the outbreak of the First World War, the government of the day demanded an increase in weapon and munition factories, Rotherwas fitted the bill exactly. The council sold the land to the ministry and by 11 July 1915, work on the new ordnance factory had begun, while the manor house was requisitioned as a barracks for the soldiers guarding the factory. Many local people including women were employed in the factory which by 1917 was producing 70,000 shells a week. After the armistice in 1918, demand decreased and only a skeleton staff remained for the purpose of breaking up unused ammunition.

The possibility that war could break out again gave the Ministry of War cause to reactivate Rotherwas in 1932. It became a filling factory for Woolwich, which eventually closed down entirely leaving Rotherwas as one of the main munitions factories in the country. A vast modernisation programme began. Alongside new buildings came a new railway link directly into the factory grounds for the transportation of finished munitions. Another necessity was the building of air raid shelters to protect the workforce should an enemy raid occur. Large earth banks arose around some of the buildings and shelters to protect them from bomb blast.

Whilst all of this work was happening, the process of employing labour began. Advertisements appeared in the *Hereford Evening News* for workers to be taken on at 'The Royal Ordnance Factory'. It did not state where, although the local people knew, but men and women

An aerial shot of the south side of Rotherwas showing the distinct layout. (Hereford Record Offiice)

A selection of Romney huts still in use at Rotherwas. (Author)

from all over the county came to sign up. One problem for the council was the lack of accommodation. Hereford, being a relatively small city, did not have sufficient housing to accommodate the influx of people wanting to work at the factory. A new estate financed by the Ministry of Supply was built which managed to house around 2,000 people from outside the area. However, with Rotherwas employing over 4,600 workers by early 1940, the problem remained. The council vainly attempted to requisition many of the larger city hotels but these had already been taken over by various government departments. In desperation they turned to another intense building programme, the result of which we can still see today on the estates surrounding Rotherwas.

The outbreak of war in 1939 brought a new sense of urgency to the factory. The site was divided in two by the road from Hereford to Holme Lacy. On one side was the North Section, which employed 2,100 people and on the other the South Section, which employed 2,500 people. Both the north and the south had a collection of buildings that were either brick-built or such as Romney huts. Most were entirely separate from each other to reduce the risk of any fire spreading should such an incident occur. Some were protected by concrete blast walls or banked-up earth mounds. The North Section housed the assembly section and was called the 'dirty' side whilst the South Section was the filling factory and was known as the 'clean' side. The work was boring and tedious but demanded extreme concentration for any mistake could prove costly.

Initially the factory was producing 3.7 inch anti-aircraft shells and later it began to manufacture 25-pounder shells. Despite being issued with protective clothing, such as long white overalls that came down to the ankles and hats that covered every inch of hair, working with the materials did have a detrimental effect on the workers. Hair would turn yellow, sometimes the skin would appear red and swollen, whilst hands would be covered in a rash. Stomach pains could be caused by inhaling TNT and sickness became a normal occurrence. People would be recognised as munitions workers just by the colour of their skin.

The plant was producing munitions 24 hours a day with three shifts coded red, white and blue. The three processes involved were the engineering factory where the shell and bomb cases were

One of the bomb-carrying rail wagons preserved for posterity at Rotherwas. (Author)

manufactured, the explosives factory where the explosives were made, and finally the filling and assembly plant. Once this process was complete the munitions were loaded onto a train that was waiting in a section of the factory with a lowered floor to be taken to the distribution centre.

Working with munitions could never be called safe. The first of several incidents at Rotherwas occurred in September 1940 when three people were killed and three were injured. One year later another explosion caused by a machine that mixed ammonium nitrate and TNT sadly killed a further three people, leaving six injured. Both these incidents were caused by faults at the factory but that cannot be said of the tragedy on Monday, 27 July 1942.

Luftwaffe activity had increased significantly around this period with many of its targets around the industrial West Midlands. Derby and Manchester were the main objectives in the early morning of the 27th when, at around 06.00 hrs, raiders were crossing the area. At Rotherwas the night shift was just finishing and in the process of clocking off, while the morning shift was arriving, when the sirens began to wail. Hundreds of men and women stopped in their tracks wondering whether to carry on or rush to the shelters. Hearing the sound of aircraft engines approaching, they looked up and saw a lone German bomber coming towards the factory. Due to it being a dull morning the blackout curtains had been taken down earlier than usual, making Rotherwas, with its main lights still on, shine like a beacon.

Rotherwas had very little in the way of defence against enemy attacks. This may seem strange, being a munitions factory and therefore a justifiable military target. It did, however, rely heavily on camouflage which from the air gave the impression of a large lake. Its sole defence was a machine gun platform, manned at most times yet on the morning of the 27th, its crew had been stood down due to perceived inactivity on the part of the Luftwaffe. Furthermore, the sole Lewis gun that was intended for low level defence had been dismantled for repairs a few days earlier.

Rotherwas did have its own platoon of the Home Guard, which included women from the factory. One such person was Barbara Fitzgerald (then Barbara Jones): 'in 1942 I was a civilian clerk in the branch of the Chief Inspectorate of Armaments in the Royal Ordnance Factory at Rotherwas. I, with two of my fellow clerks, joined the Home Guard, some of the men on site already being members. We were not issued with a uniform but had badges with HG printed on them. They

This was the 3rd Herefordshire (City) Battalion (note several female members). (T. Townsend)

were made of wood or plaster and were coloured gold. We had instruction on firing the guns, carried out lying on the floor of an empty building. Early morning training was carried out on Dinedor Hill close by which was often covered in frost and fog. I remember the plane that dropped the bombs but at that time the guns were not active due to maintenance. It was flying very low and the noise of its engines was deafening.'

Flying very low over the factory, two 250kg bombs were dropped from the Dornier 17. One landed on a transit shed, in the process killing 17 workers and injuring a further 24. The second bomb was deflected by the concrete surface and bounced over the factory perimeter, tragically killing five family members of the factory police superintendent, Mr Ernest Hursey.

Brian Thomas, a Hereford resident, relates the story: 'although Rotherwas was bombed on only one occasion, the general opinion was that the German bombers which occasionally flew up the Wye Valley were searching for it. Numerous bombs were jettisoned in the area, possibly in the hope of hitting the target. From the air Rotherwas was well camouflaged and in the moonlight appeared

I have received The King's command to express His Majesty's appreciation of the loyal service given voluntarily to her country in a time of grievous danger by

BARBARA ANN JONES.

as a Woman Home Guard Auxiliary.

The War Office,
London.

Secretary of State
for War

The letter of appreciation received by Barbara Jones after the war in recognition of her service in the Home Guard while at Rotherwas. (Barbara Fitzgerald) to be a large lake. The river Wye was an excellent navigational aid to the enemy but it was said that with the factory being tucked in close to Dinedor Hill, low-flying aircraft would quickly pass over the target area.

'On the morning of the day of the raid, the lone raider which I think was a Dornier 17, flew up the Wye Valley at a very low altitude. A farmer at Poulstone, Kings Caple, remarked at the time "he was so low I could have touched him with a long pole". Some of the men arrived on one of the buses for the start of the early morning shift only to find the factory gates locked. Without having time to rattle the gates or ring the bell, they saw the aircraft coming in very low over the Cathedral towards them. It is said that as some of them dived into the roadside ditch, they could see a member of the crew waving to them! Another female employee who lived in Mortimer Road, which is on a direct route from the Cathedral, was able to describe what a member of the crew was wearing, so low was the aircraft. Doris Evans of Little Dewchurch was working in No 3 Section when one of the bombs came in through one side of the shed and out through the other without exploding. Minutes later the second bomb did explode. As for the bomber, apparently it was heading home having dropped its bombs when it was intercepted by Spitfires from Tern Hill airfield in Shropshire. The Dornier 17 was shot down and crashed somewhere over south Gloucestershire. I was told that the Germans were unaware that the factory they had bombed was a Royal Ordnance Factory. Luckily they did not hit the explosives area or many more would have been killed.'

The first official to arrive on the scene minutes later was the head warden of the local ARP group. He found the Hurseys' house demolished with parts of it in flames. Calling out, he heard a voice from amongst the debris and clearing some of the rubble, found one of the young sons alive. He was the only survivor. The warden, who had by now been joined by several others, remained on the site until 04.00 hrs to ensure that no-one else was unaccounted for. When the fires were brought under control, many people from the surrounding villages arrived to see what had happened. This was to hamper the clear-up operation and troops from a local unit were sent in to clear the area. Much of the power to the factory was cut off, causing the inner doors to lock automatically, thus shutting down much of the machinery and not letting workers into the factory. Only several days later when total power was restored could Rotherwas get back fully into production.

A consignment of bombs arrives at a storage depot – a scene similar to that at Rotherwas. (SE Newspapers)

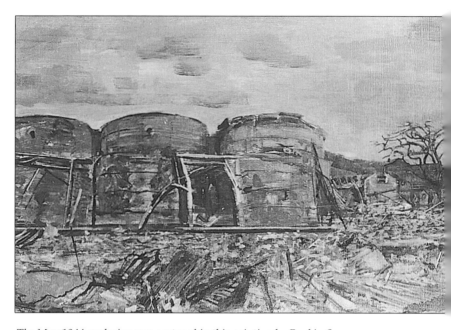

The May 1944 explosion was captured in this painting by Ruskin Spear.
(Ruskin Spear, via Imperial War Museum.)

This was the only time that Rotherwas was hit by the Luftwaffe. Local people have said that they remember a formation of bombers flying up the Monnow Valley a few weeks earlier and reaching Abergavenny before turning round and returning to scatter their bombs across the countryside. It is assumed that the aircraft had followed the wrong river and that Rotherwas, which is by the River Wye, was their intended target. Such was the impact of the factory bombing that Clement Attlee, a member of the War Cabinet, travelled to Hereford to see the damage for himself. Touring the factory he remarked on the high spirits of the men and women working there. During his stay he was told it was thought the reason why the first bomb did not explode was due to the fact that it had no fuse inserted. Other rumours at the time suggested that the enemy aircraft was so low the bomb did not have time to land upright but skated along on its side.

In October 1942 another in-house explosion was to shake the factory, resulting in two further deaths and four injuries. This time it happened

in a shell-filling house where men and women were loading filled and fused shells onto a trolley to await transportation to the train trucks.

With the war now going the Allies' way, 1944 saw much of the armaments production going over to 5,000 lb bombs and naval mines. It was the latter that were the cause of the largest explosion at Rotherwas, which killed two people and badly injured several more. 30th May was a hot summer's day. It was the Whitsun weekend but, although a public holiday, around 2,700 people, 2,000 of them women, were working. Production of the mines was at full bore and once they had been filled and primed, they awaited the train trucks to transport them to the distribution depots. The strong sun streaming through the window was concentrated on one mine which for some reason began to emit smoke. Realising what was happening, one of the factory workers had the sense to push the fire alarm sending a bell ringing throughout the factory. Three men working in the section, Mr Little, Mr Tyler and Mr Morris attempted to put out the smoking mine with sand and water to allow the rest of the section to get out to the shelters.

Address presented to the Royal Ordnance Factory, Rotherwas, on the 22nd March, 1945.

The address presented to the Royal Ordnance Factory, Rotherwas on 22 March 1945, recognising the bravery of those caught up in the 1944 explosion.

The destruction of German cities was one result of the work at Rotherwas. (Crown)

The fire alarm had alerted the emergency services in Hereford as well as the factory services, both rushing to the scene at once. Fire engines, ambulances and the police stood by as the three men continued in their efforts to stop the mine from expanding. Suddenly at around 6 pm the casing, no longer able to absorb the pressure, split and seconds later the mine exploded. The resulting pressure threw the men some distance away, sadly killing Mr Morris and badly injuring the other two. Fire engulfed the building and while the firemen were wrestling with the inferno, another explosion occurred when the remaining bombs close by blew up. With this the entire building collapsed, causing major injuries to many. Although surrounded by carnage the services were beginning to get the situation under control when a third but lesser explosion occurred. This aggravated the situation but gradually the fires were brought under control.

An account of the incident was recorded by the daughter of one of the factory employees: 'My father was a fireman at the Royal Ordnance Factory. We lived in a row of firemen's houses at Rotherwas during the time of the major bomb explosion. A fire started with a large bomb and then gradually spread to other bombs, mines and an incorporater filled with explosive. My father was awarded the BEM for his courage and devotion to duty with many others receiving commendations. He and his mate were working on the bomb and adjacent ones when the first explosion occurred. It knocked him over backwards and he was badly cut about the head. Whilst my father was helping his badly injured mate, the second explosion occurred. Living so near to the factory, it blew out all our windows and doors which were not replaced properly for ages.'

The fires were brought under control by 8 pm that evening. It was later estimated that the equivalent of 31 mines and 2,000 lb bombs had exploded on that one day. Although clearance of rubble went on for many days, the factory soon got back to full production. The bravery of some of the men and women over this and the other incidents was recognised by several awards with investitures at Buckingham Palace.

From this time until the end of the war no other incidents were recorded. After May 1945, mass production of munitions ceased and instead of making shells and bombs, the process was reversed and they were taken apart. This continued until Rotherwas finally closed on 29 September 1945. The Ministry of Supply then used part of the site to break up tanks and bren gun carriers.

There is no doubt the munitions factories were vital to the winning of the war. In addition to making shells and bombs, the women workers boosted the morale of the men in the forces by slipping notes into the cases of armaments 'so the soldiers knew we were thinking of them'. Gestures like this brought out the human side of what was a dirty and dangerous job.

Rotherwas still abounds with wartime buildings though the entire area is now a huge industrial site. Some units have luckily decided to keep their wartime appearance for the sake of history, but the name Rotherwas will always be synonymous with munitions.

Wolverhampton (Boulton Paul)

When it appeared on 11 August 1937, the Defiant fighter aircraft represented a new concept since it was the first in the world to dispense with fixed forward-firing machine guns, and it was also Boulton Paul's first aircraft incorporating an all-metal stressed skin.

A Boulton Paul Defiant of No 256 Squadron. Defiants were manufactured at Wolver-hampton. (MAP)

For armament it used a power-operated turret behind the cockpit. The concept was, however, short-lived. Designed to specification F.9/35, the Defiant entered service early in 1940 and after a brief period of glory was relegated to night-fighting in August 1941. Although some measure of success was achieved in this role, compared with other night-fighters of a later period it was minimal. By the spring of 1942, most Defiants were being used for target-towing duties. This was the one and only wartime aircraft that Boulton Paul were to design and build although they were sub-contracted to build several Fleet Air Arm (FAA) aircraft.

With the interest in civic aerodromes proliferating during the 1930s, Wolverhampton was intent on not being left behind. An area known as Dunstall Park was chosen but plans to develop the site as a municipal airfield were not to see the light of day. Many years later a Norwich-based company named Boulton & Paul which had been making aircraft during the First World War decided to sell off its aircraft department. Renaming itself Boulton Paul Aircraft Ltd, in 1934 the department moved to a new factory site at Pendeford, Wolverhampton.

With the design of the Defiant still on the drawing board, one of the first contracts offered to the company was that of building the Hawker Demon. The main Hawker factory at Kingston in Surrey could not sustain the production required by the Air Ministry and so was forced to sub-contract work to other aviation companies.

The first aircraft built at Wolverhampton flew on 21 August 1936. This was a standard Hawker design but from October of that year, all Demons from the factory were fitted with a Frazer-Nash hydraulic turret. This was to be the first venture by Boulton Paul into fixed turret armament. However, restrictions placed by the government's penchant for secrecy prevented the company from selling the turrets elsewhere. At the same time a French-designed turret known as the de Boysson had raised little interest with the French government. Boulton Paul were allowed to acquire sole rights to develop and manufacture it within the British Isles. Two prototypes were produced with provision for either two or four machine guns or a 20 mm cannon. It was the latter that offered the most potential when installed in bombers and experiments were therefore carried out using an Overstrand bomber. In April 1935 a specification, F.9/35, was issued for a two-seat day and night fighter. Boulton Paul produced a design incorporating the new turret, though this time fitted with four 0.303 Browning machine guns. The company named the aircraft the Defiant.

The prototype Defiant (K8310) flew from Pendeford on 11 August 1937 powered by a Rolls-Royce Merlin I engine. Two years later the first production aircraft (L6950) flew on 30 July 1939 fitted with the by-then standard Merlin III engine. With handling characteristics proving favourable, mass production of the Defiant began. The original contract was for 87 aircraft but with this number entering service between August 1939 and May 1940, an extended contract was issued by the Ministry, the total order reaching 1,064 before production ceased in February 1943.

First to receive the new type was No 264 Squadron at Martlesham Heath. They used the Defiant to good effect, shooting down 65 enemy aircraft, mainly over the Dunkirk period (May 1940). This success was, however, short-lived once the enemy realised that the power-operated turret had a blind spot near the tail due to the fact that it could not fire downwards. Losses began to climb alarmingly, so much so that by August 1940, it was decided to withdraw the Defiant from daylight operations.

It now entered a new lease of life as a night-fighter equipped with AI radar (designed at Malvern and tested at Defford). It did well and was

The production floor for the Blackburn Roc at the Boulton Paul works. (Mark Ansell)

to obtain the highest number of 'kills' per interception of any night-fighter type in the winter of 1940/41. Thirteen night-fighter squadrons flew Defiants, the original Mk Is slowly being replaced by Mk IIs.

Boulton Paul at Wolverhampton continued to build the Defiant until 1943. Whilst the factory occupied the major part of the airfield, it was also used by No 28 Elementary Flying Training School (EFTS). The demand for pilots accelerated during 1941 and the Ministry opted to open further training schools. No 28 was formed on 1 September 1941 under the control of 51 Group FTC. Thirty Tiger Moths came on strength with a further 36 being added in May 1942 when No 17 EFTS at Peterborough closed. With so many movements taking place it was necessary for Wolverhampton to be allocated two relief landing grounds. These were situated at Battlestead Hill and Penkridge.

Although the town of Wolverhampton with its industrial factories was attacked several times, no bombs fell on the airfield. This allowed the production and training facilities to continue uninterrupted. The

Sub-contracted to Boulton Paul Aircraft, the Blackburn Roc. (Mark Ansell)

never-ending need for pilots saw many Turkish Air Force officers arrive for training. Aware that neutral Turkey could enter the war on the side of the Axis forces, a personal intervention by Churchill won a contract to train these men.

The EFTS was to continue to the end of the war when it was renumbered No 25 RFS. With the production of the Defiant finally ending in February 1943, the company went on to build 105 Blackburn Rocs and 692 Fairey Barracudas, both aircraft for use with the FAA. The manufacture of the Roc was entrusted entirely to Boulton Paul whilst the Barracuda was sub-contracted to the company.

Peacetime saw Wolverhampton become a thriving civil airport though not on a municipal scale. Wolverhampton Aero Club was established while the RFS continued and Boulton Paul were busy building the Balliol trainer for the RAF as well as converting 270 Wellington bombers to T10 navigation trainers. In addition, the company carried out modification work on the English Electric Canberra and de Havilland Vampire as well as becoming a sub-contractor for Beagle Aircraft. Later, taxi-ing trials on the P.III and P.120

Delta research aircraft were carried out at Wolverhampton. However, with the rapid advances in jet aircraft, the company moved to Seighford in 1956.

The 1960s saw Wolverhampton in rapid decline and a tragic accident on 9 April 1970 when a de Havilland Dove crashed, killing three people, finally forced the council to close the airport. In 1961 Boulton Paul joined the Dowty Group, to become solely an aircraft component manufacturer. Once closed, Wolverhampton went the way of most wartime airfields, to be replaced by housing. Sadly, very little is left to remind us of another great British aircraft manufacturer.

12
CIVILIANS AT WAR

A wireless announcement broadcast at 11 am on Sunday, 3 September 1939 sent a chill through every British household. It warned listeners to stand by for an important speech by the Prime Minister. Immediately after the announcement, the popular singer of the time, Parry Jones, sang *As ever I saw*, followed by a rendering of *Di Ballo* by the London Symphony Orchestra. In the capital, Downing Street became full of people waiting for news. At 11.21 am, Neville Chamberlain made his broadcast advising the public that Britain was now at war with Germany. It is recorded that minutes after, the King at Buckingham Palace opened a new diary entry: 'The country is calm, firm and united behind its leaders, resolved to fight until liberty and justice are once more safe in the world.'

Chamberlain's speech was followed by the National Anthem, the end of which was drowned by the wailing of air raid sirens in London, East Anglia and parts of the Midlands. At 11.48 am the 'All Clear' was sounded. The aircraft plotted crossing the Kent coast was not hostile but bringing two French officers to London. At 12 noon the House of Commons met, only the fourth time in history that it had done so on a Sunday. At 12.06 pm, Neville Chamberlain rose in the House and declared, 'this is a sad day for all of us and to none is it sadder than to me.'

For Winston Churchill, sitting waiting to be called by the Speaker, all his warnings had now come to pass: 'as I sat in my place listening to the speeches, a very strong sense of calm came over me, after the intense passions and excitements of the last few days. The glory of Old England, peace-loving and ill-prepared as she was, but instant and fearless at the call of honour, thrilled my being and seemed to lift our fate to those spheres far removed from earthly facts and physical sensation. I tried to convey some of this mood to the House when I spoke.' Despite all the efforts by politicians

'Peace in our time': Neville Chamberlain holds the infamous paper in his hand. (Crown)

and military men, Britain was once again on the edge of a vast abyss.

Though the air raid sirens did sound in areas of the West Midlands on Sunday, 3 September, it is not recorded whether they were heard in Herefordshire or Worcestershire. Certainly, far from the battle front, the two counties were to be spared much of the Blitz but the citizens were to face the difficulties that war brought as well as experiencing death and destruction. It was felt that an attack could come at any time. Emergency Order 504 stated that anyone could be drafted to do any task needed for meeting enemy action. The people of the two counties were ready to do their best to aid the war effort.

Before we look at the personal effects of war on the civilians of the two counties, we must consider the difficulties that every family in the land had to endure. Three days after war was declared the process of evacuation began, code-named 'Operation Pied Piper'. Many parents were forced to entrust the livelihood and safety of their children to strangers. It was the coming together of two different cultures, urban transferred to rural. Herefordshire and Worcestershire were considered safe areas and so many children were evacuated from London to the Midlands countryside. They arrived complete with gas masks carried in little cardboard boxes, small suitcases and the inevitable label giving their name, address and age.

For many of the local people, this was quite a shock as Margaret Wilce from Ross-on-Wye remembers: 'the first evacuees that came to the village were from London. Ross was really only a country town and I was terrified as I had never seen a black person before and there was a whole family. The other children were so boisterous and many had terrible sores (impetigo). I soon fell over and had the same sores: mother spent hours bathing the scabs off then rubbing ointment in. When they eventually healed, I often fell down and the whole process started all over again. Quite a few evacuees came to Ross but many of them returned to their own homes when nothing happened at the beginning of the war.'

In September 1939, 827,000 schoolchildren, 524,000 pre-school children and their mothers, 12,000 pregnant women and 103,000 teachers and helpers were on the move, a tremendous upheaval for one month alone. The government had planned to move about 3.5 million people but in the end only 1.5 million families joined the scheme. However, during the quiet period known as the 'Phoney War' three out of four children returned to their families. Despite this, evacuation continued throughout the war and in

Children in gas masks. The threat of a gas attack was always considered a possibility. (Crown)

Tearful farewells as the children are evacuated. (SE Newspapers)

addition to the national figure, more than 70,000 evacuated children were sent abroad.

On the domestic front however, the effects of rationing were to hit every household. It was first introduced in January 1940, but the government had been stockpiling ration cards since 1938. Almost immediately butter, sugar, bacon and ham were rationed, followed by meat in March. Offal, fish and bread were left untouched although in 1942 the normal white loaf was replaced by the very unpopular 'national wheatmeal loaf'. Later in the war a points system was applied to canned meat, fish and vegetables. Under this system each person had 20 points which had to last for four weeks. Between the summers of 1940 and 1941, many ships carrying foodstuffs to Britain were sunk. The arrival, however, of the first American lend/lease goods provided the housewife with versatile canned meats, especially Spam. Little luxuries had arrived at long last!

Overall, housewives had to cope with immense difficulties as a result of wartime shortages. As the queues got longer so, somehow, a sense of optimism and good humour became prevalent. Every woman was committed to make sacrifices if it was to help the country win the war.

To help feed the populace, people were encouraged to 'dig for victory' which entailed digging up lawns and large areas of open land in order to plant and grow vegetables. Another contribution that was to help the situation was the introduction of the Women's Land Army. First appearing during the First World War, it was reformed in June 1939 under the leadership of the Marquis of Reading. In the drive for self-sufficiency, the WLA were at the forefront. Dressed in a uniform consisting of brown dungarees or corduroy britches together with a green pullover, they were to fill the huge gap left by male farm workers who had been conscripted. Toiling from dawn to dusk, they carried out such work as milking and general farm labouring, planting and collecting vegetables and helping with threshing at harvest time, (a particularly dusty job).

It was not all hard work however as one particular Land Army recruit recalled: 'I joined the WLA in March 1942. I received my uniform at home. Trying on the corduroy breeches was a laugh, they were laced at the knees and trying to bend my legs was difficult. There were knee-length woollen stockings, brown leather shoes, cream shirts, green jumpers, a lovely three-quarter length dark beige coat with white wool lining, beige hat and a wide leather belt. We got the rest, wellies, overalls, big oilskin macs etc when we got to the hostel.

Women operating a range predictor somewhere in the Midlands. (SE Newspapers)

'My destination was Leominster in Herefordshire, we had never heard of the place never having been any further than Scarborough or Bridlington. When we arrived at the station my brothers said, "There's a compartment with some more land girls in so come on." I said my goodbyes to them and settled in my seat. We were all looking at each other so I said, "I'm going to Leominster, where are you going?" Imagine what I felt when they said that they were going there as well. By the end of the journey we had all become good friends. We were met at the station by a smart lady with her utility van. She told us she was our clerk driver, she would be driving us to the farms where we were to do field work. We were to live in a hostel in the village of Kingsland, the hostel being a single-storied wooden building standing in a field. It was very primitive but I eventually got used to it. Miss Freeman, the landowner, was very nice but she seemed a bit "posh" to us northern lasses. She took us round to meet some of the farmers who were not too keen to have girls working on their farms even though we were cheap labour. They must have thought we would not last, us town girls around five feet two inches tall and weighing about eight stone.

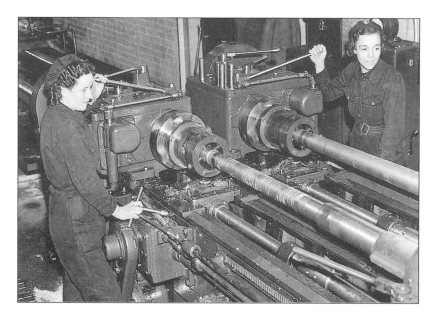

Women at work in a heavy engineering factory. (SE Newspapers)

'Our jobs were many and varied – hoeing, oh so boring! Thistle bodging, stone picking, hay making, stacking corn, building hay and wheat ricks, loading the carts and leading the horses for ploughing. I was leading Blossom and Daisy one day and as I was turning them at the end of the row, one of them trod on my foot. The great big carthorse didn't heed my frantic efforts so I shouted to the ploughman, "The bugger's on my foot." He just laughed but managed to move the horse.

'Herefordshire was a lovely county, all the seasons had their own beauty. I remember Dinmore Hill going into Hereford in autumn with all the trees red and gold. It was a lovely sight. Best of all in my eyes was springtime when the apple blossom was out. It looked really beautiful. We were never short of company in the evening with an airfield for glider pilots nearby (Shobdon). Later on the Americans came and were stationed in the area. The first time we saw them we thought they were all officers, their uniforms were so smart compared to the RAF. They were like film stars and had badges for everything. Both they and the RAF brightened our lives and I have no doubt that we would do it all again, even though now I have arthritis in my knees and hips and an aching, aching back.'

By 1942 mechanisation had arrived in the form of tractors. Despite the fact that the year had seen the number of tractors available increase to 150,000, many wanted to continue farming the traditional way with horse-drawn appliances.

It was not only on the land that women were to work. As we have read, at Rotherwas many worked in the munitions factories. Some went into heavy engineering and helped to build aeroplanes, ships and tanks whilst others served in Civil Defence. December 1941 saw the conscription of women, initially between the ages of 20 and 30. They were given the option of choosing what industry they would like to work in. Many chose the auxiliary services, the WRNS, WAAFs and the ATS. The age limit was raised to 50 in 1943 but married women living with their husbands and women with children under 14 were exempt.

When it came to Civil Defence, the recruits were once again mainly volunteers. Given the job of keeping civil order when all around was falling down, together with the local constable, the air raid wardens would direct people to shelters when a raid was imminent. When it

The Marden Home Guard at Marden Court in 1940. (SE Newspapers)

Battle of Britain Week in Hereford, circa 1943 (M. Beauchamp via D. Foxton).

had passed, theirs was the duty of entering bombed buildings to look for signs of life. The butt of many a comedian's jokes, the phrase 'Put that b----light out' became their catchword. Civil Defence included the Auxiliary Fire Service, later the National Fire Service, and the ambulance service. They too had the task of looking for bodies or signs of life in bombed out buildings.

For those who wished to remain in their own homes there was added protection with the erection of an Anderson shelter in the garden or a Morrison shelter within the house. The former, designed by Dr D.A. Anderson, was usually semi-sunk in the garden with further added protection offered by sandbags placed alongside and across the entrance. The shelter was issued free to all earning less than £250 a year and at a charge of £7 for those on higher incomes. Eventually 2,250,000 were erected, some remaining *in situ* to this day. The Morrison shelter was usually installed in the main living room of a house. It was a metal table upon which one could eat meals with the sides encased in strong metal mesh within which one slept. (The author remembers well the experience of attempting sleep in a Morrison shelter!)

A Home Guard demonstration 'somewhere in the Midlands'. (SE Newspapers)

Though officially a military-based organisation, the Home Guard was another form of civil defence first proposed by Churchill, then First Lord of the Admiralty, in October 1939, who suggested a force of 500,000 men be formed. Not much happened at the time but seven months later, when Churchill became Prime Minister, Anthony Eden, a minister in the War Cabinet, made this appeal on the radio:

'Since the war began the Government has received countless inquiries from all over the kingdom from men of all ages who are for one reason or another not at present engaged in military service, and who wish to do something for the defence of their country. Well, now is your opportunity. We want large numbers of such men in Great Britain, who are British subjects, between the ages of 17 and 65 to come forward now and offer their services. The name of the new force which is now to be raised will be "The Local Defence Volunteers".'

Almost immediately volunteers were registering at their local police stations. Within 24 hours, 250,000 men had enrolled and by June 1940, this had risen to 1.5 million. Although known at first as the LDV, it quickly became known as the Home Guard after Winston Churchill had referred to this civilian organisation in one of his speeches. Many recruits had seen service during the First World War and were eager to do their bit once again. Despite the promise that 'you will be issued with a uniform and arms', the first volunteers were issued only with armbands plus a variety of ancient wooden implements, mainly pickaxe handles, broom handles and hoes. An appeal for firearms brought forward a motley selection of ancient guns including some from the gunroom at Sandringham. Later a consignment of rifles from America, albeit also old, did give the force some ability to tackle the enemy should he invade. The standard army uniform was issued later in 1940 to all personnel and by the summer of 1943 the Home Guard had swollen to 1,100 battalions with a total personnel of 1.75 million. The size of the units depended mainly on what areas they were to cover and protect. One battalion of the twelve formed in Worcestershire was known as the Worcester City Battalion and was initially solely responsible for guarding Perdiswell airfield against aerial or ground attack, a duty that was later taken on by the newly formed RAF Regiment. Several units were formed in Herefordshire, most of them with their headquarters located in a local public house.

Bob Greenhill, the son of one of the recruiters, explains: 'once the Germans had broken through the Maginot Line and the BEF were all but trapped, the outlook for our country was grim. Somehow, though, it sent a sense of unity and defiance through the nation. My father, a

Kington in Herefordshire supported an unusual horse-mounted battalion of the Home Guard.

head gardener at one of the big estates, went around the village community recruiting men with shotguns. He had no difficulty in organising the Local Defence Force when it was known that the headquarters was to be the village pub, the Trumpet Inn. At this critical time it was best to keep a sharp lookout so a well known

vantage point was chosen, this being the upstairs room of the pub! The LDV consisted mainly of farm workers who were issued with armbands. They dug trenches and, knowing every bit of the neighbourhood, travelled around on bicycles. Besides shotguns some of the men had .22 rifles whilst some just had pickaxe handles. Other units were set up in the villages around, causing some animosity when men were "poached" from the "Trumpet Platoon" to form the "Crown Platoon". My father, Lieutenant Greenhill, was the only one issued with a uniform straight away and I remember my mother pressing it and sewing on his pips and shoulder flashes denoting "HOME GUARD". Although most of the men from the village joined, the local blacksmith refused and whilst the men were on duty on cold and wet nights, he was comfortable in bed. Not standing for this, some of the men fired shots into the air outside his house. Thinking that the Germans had arrived, he rushed to the window to be greeted by shouts of "At least that got the bugger up"!

'When the uniform was finally issued to all the men it consisted of a forage cap, battle dress, greatcoat, leather belt and gaiters. They were later issued with elderly .300 American rifles which were covered in grease from where they had lain in the unopened boxes for years. My father had to give up the church where he was the choirmaster as regular Sunday training with drill and lectures began to take up all his time. There is no doubt, however, that both his and all the other platoons at places such as Bishopswood and Walford, Bishops Frome and Hereford City, who had their headquarters at the Rose and Crown pub in Ledbury Road, were ready to do their bit if it ever came to invasion.'

One of the more unusual units of home defence in Herefordshire was known as the 'Much Marcle Watchers'. Formed before Eden's speech, the unit came about when Lady Helena Gleichen, a distinguished artist and relative of King George VI, walked into the headquarters of the Shropshire Light Infantry at Ross-on-Wye and asked for 80 rifles together with ammunition. She added that she could do with some machine guns as well in order to form a defence force. Stunned by this outrageous request, the officers stuttered that no guns were available and even if this were not the case they would not let her have any. Undefeated, Lady Helena went ahead and gathered together a force of men armed with an armoury of shotguns including Austrian rifles and bayonets taken from her own collection of guns. That same night the 'Much Marcle Watchers' were on duty ready to defend their beloved Herefordshire, the forerunners of the yet to be formed Home Guard.

In addition to the Home Guard battalions, mobile columns were also formed. Worcestershire had three in total, one at Malvern, one at Redditch and another at Hagley. These were in addition to the regular army counter-attack columns which were formed and based at No 23

Infantry Training Centre at Norton Barracks. At its peak the county had recruited 20,000 men. In North Herefordshire volunteers topped all the 110 battalions in the Western Command Area, a fact that was 'mentioned in despatches' after the war. The Home Guard was unique to Britain and there is no doubt that had the enemy invaded, 'Dad's Army' would have been in the forefront of the national defence.

Similar to the Home Guard though endeavouring to keep a lower profile were the men of the GHQ Auxiliary Units, sometimes known as the GHQ Reserve. A British secret resistance organisation, their role had the Germans invaded was to carry out acts of sabotage behind enemy lines. A further duty was to create havoc and destruction among the enemy's supplies and communications. Very little has ever been written about the auxiliary units that were formed in 1940 at the same time as the Home Guard. Its members were recruited mostly from the farming community and those in reserve occupations, organised into patrols of about six men who knew the area thoroughly. Herefordshire and Worcestershire established something like twelve patrols. Even today very little is known or recorded about their activities yet if the enemy had invaded, no doubt the units would have offered stiff resistance.

The chief medium that kept the civilian population informed of what was happening in the war was the radio. At the outbreak of war, regional programmes were shut down and it was left to the single BBC Home Service to inform the populace. Radio also played its part in raising morale with programmes such as *ITMA*, *Music While You Work*, *Workers' Playtime* and many others. In any one week, 16 million people were to tune into *ITMA* with Tommy Handley, Arthur Askey and Richard 'Stinker' Murdoch. The catchphrases 'Don't forget the diver' and 'Can I do you now sir? were to become national bywords. It was, however, the news at 9 pm that became the most important time of the day. Read in turn by Alvar Liddell, Bruce Belfrage or Wilfred Pickles, it told of disasters and triumphs as the war progressed. Countless families lived the war through the radio broadcasts and for the people of Europe, it was the voice of freedom.

One voice that attracted a rather less large radio audience in Britain was that of 'Lord Haw Haw'. William Joyce, a former member of the British Union of Fascists, had offered his services to the Nazis at the beginning of the war. The nickname was derived from an article in a September 1939 issue of the *Daily Express*, referring to a broadcaster who had a rather 'upper class' accent. When Joyce began broadcasting by announcing 'Jairmany Calling, Jairmany Calling' in a parody of an

227

The Drum and Bugle Band of the 3rd Herefordshire (City) Battalion at the stand-down in 1944. (T. McVeigh)

upper class accent with nasal distortions, the name stuck. He continued his propaganda broadcasts until the end of the war when he was arrested by the British and hanged for treason. The radio, however, did bring the people of Herefordshire and Worcestershire the news of the London Blitz and all that it involved during late 1940.

So far from the main battle front, Herefordshire only experienced sporadic bombing. This is not to say it was any less dangerous as the Rotherwas bombs showed. Though that was considered the major bombing incident in this area, raiders dropped bombs at random throughout the county, mainly over the abundance of countryside that surrounds the towns. Many enemy aircraft returning home from bombing Birmingham, Nottingham and other Midlands cities were glad to jettison what bombs they had left just about anywhere.

Ross-on-Wye and environs seemed to receive many of these bombs, the first of which is recorded as falling on the night of 2 July 1940 making craters at Old Gore. Some fell along the riverbank at Bishops-wood whilst others fell on Ley's Hill. Memories of these incidents were recalled by Mrs Margaret Wilce in a letter to the local paper:

'My father, when he wasn't taking the gates and railings off the residents of the town for the war effort, was an ARP warden at Walford. He often said that Hitler was trying to bomb the factory at Lydbrook (Edison Swan Cables), which during the First World War made munitions. Every time the siren sounded in Ross, father would put his ARP uniform and tin hat on. He recalled the bombs falling along the river bank at Bishopswood and on another occasion he was on guard when he saw the enemy plane coming towards him. He shouted, not to anyone in particular, "Look out, he's opened his bomb doors", and there followed the loudest explosion imaginable. How-ever, it was not until the next day when someone was walking from Coughton to Howle Hill that an enormous crater was found in woodland behind Howle Hill church.

'One night the siren sounded when father was in the garden. Looking up he shouted, "the searchlights at Coppett Hill have got him", then minutes later, "he's British and he has bailed out". The searchlight followed the airman down into the trees at Bishopswood and although father tried to find him, he had disappeared. The story of what had happened rapidly spread around the area and the bravery of a young girl was revealed. Apparently the airman, despite the pitch blackness, had found his way out of Oxlet Wood to the Chadwyns' farmhouse. The daughter of the house took the airman, through dark narrow lanes and with the threat of bombs falling, to the nearest

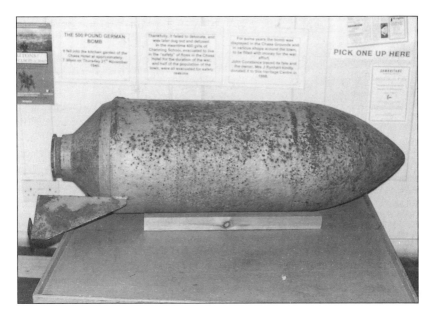

The 500 lb bomb dropped on Ross on Wye on 21 November 1940. (B. Thomas)

telephone at the Queach Ley's Hill, then the home of Major Gaskell Davies, whereupon he was able to contact his unit. My mother was extremely disappointed father hadn't found the parachute as she was a good needle-woman and would have made good use of the silk panels.'

According to another publication there were 146 high explosive bombs, two oil bombs and hundreds of incendiaries dropped in the Ross area. The only one actually to fall on the town did not explode. It was a 500 pounder which landed in the kitchen garden just 200 yds from the Chase Hotel, the wartime home of 400 girls from Channing School. The bomb fell at 7.30 on the evening of Thursday, 21 November 1940 but its whereabouts were not known until the next morning. Nearby houses and the hotel were evacuated when the Bomb Disposal team arrived to make the device safe. This particular bomb is now on show in the Ross Heritage Centre.

Closer to the city of Hereford was an incident remembered by Trevor Watkins, then a nine-year-old boy: 'it was either at the end of 1940 or in the early months of 1941 that a chance bomb attack happened in the Credenhill area. No records have survived to my knowledge and it receives no mention in any records of the war years relating to Herefordshire as far as I know. As members of my family including myself had a narrow escape, I can vouch for the facts.

'My mother and father together with my brother were walking home to Credenhill from the nearby village of Kenchester where we had attended evening chapel service. It was a Sunday evening around 7 pm, very dark and no lights showing due to the blackout. We paused for a while as my father and my uncle, who was accompanying us part of the way home, discussed the identity of an approaching low-flying aircraft. I remember that my uncle was of the opinion that it was British while my father was certain it was German. A screaming whistle terminated the discussion as something passed above us, my father and uncle throwing my mother, brother and myself into a nearby ditch. After a few minutes we emerged very shaken but unharmed and not having heard any explosion we assumed that we were in close proximity to an unexploded bomb. We ran most of the rest of the way home, passing one or two villagers who had heard an explosion and were out of doors anxiously wondering what had happened.

'The following morning we received an early visit from the local policeman who had been told that we were near to the scene the previous evening. He assured my parents that the bomb had exploded and it was now safe. It was when we passed by later on our way to school that we realised our narrow escape. The bomb had missed the road and the nearby farm buildings by about twenty yards before exploding in deep mud and mire. Unable to see properly in the dark, we had run almost through the edge of the crater. The explosion was heard some distance away but it did not register with us. It was assumed that the mud etc had to some extent nullified the effects of the blast, the farm buildings only suffering superficial damage. Just how lucky can you be?'

Many incidents within the borders of Herefordshire involved aircraft crashes. With a number of OTUs situated in the area, trainee pilots were constantly at risk from mechanical failure and also weather conditions. The mist-shrouded mountains of Wales just touching the fringes of the county were also to become a graveyard of crashed aircraft. One such incident resulted in the loss of a well known vicar and his church organist in bizarre circumstances.

In July 1942, No 21 OTU were operating Wellingtons from Moreton-in-Marsh, an airfield situated in the neighbouring county of Glou-cestershire. One particular aircraft, Wellington Ic T2962, was detailed for a cross-country training flight late in the afternoon of 7th July. The all-sergeant crew took off from Moreton at approximately 16.30 hrs in good weather. Twenty-five minutes into the flight the pilot, Sgt F.H.S. Bush, noticed that one of the engines was not fully functioning. Minutes later it seized up and losing height, he desperately looked for a clear area upon which to crash-land. Unfortunately the aircraft became unstable and crashed into the churchyard at Christ Church, Llangrove. In the resultant fire, Sgt Bush and another crew member, Sgt R.J. McKean, died with the remaining four crew members injured.

With the aircraft crashing and bursting into flames, before long many local people were running to the scene to offer what assistance they could to the wounded crew who had managed to escape from the aircraft. They included the vicar, the Reverend Frank Easton. Administering what comfort he could over many hours, the strain of this harrowing experience became too much and whilst returning to his vicarage on his bicycle some time later, he collapsed and died instantly. Likewise his organist, Mrs Watkins, who had assisted in carrying buckets of war from the church in order to help quench burning parts of the aircraft, stumbled in the roadway and fell down. She was taken to a nearby cottage suffering from exhaustion and she died shortly after. It was a tragedy that Llangrove has never forgotten.

The crash of a Stirling bomber at Rosemaund Farm, Preston Wynne is remembered by a plaque placed in the local church and dedicated to the memory of the nine airmen who lost their lives. The Stirling, E352, of No 1657 Heavy Conversion Unit crashed during bad weather at 21.20 hrs on 22 October 1943. With the aircraft exploding on impact, sadly there were no survivors. What remained of the bodies were taken to RAF Hereford (Credenhill) for identification and burial.

It was not only British aircraft that were to fall within Herefordshire's borders. In August 1944, an American B24 Liberator of the 406th Bomb Squadron based at Cheddington in Buckinghamshire crashed in flames after striking two chimneys of St Mary's Mental Hospital at Burghill. It then hit a wall near the institution reservoir before finally coming to rest in a field. Eight members of the crew were killed whilst two more survived. The patients had a fortunate escape for most of the debris from one of the chimneys completely covered the only unoccupied bed in the ward. Fire units from Hereford and nearby villages who tackled the inferno risked danger from exploding ammunition as they fought to bring the fire in the aircraft under control.

'One that did not return', photographed 'somewhere in the Midlands'. (Crown)

These examples of death from the sky are but a few of many recorded incidents in the county. The bombing of Rotherwas munitions factory may have been the only planned attack by the Luftwaffe on a military target in Hereford but a similar attack was carried out on another military target in the city of Worcester on Tuesday, 3 October 1940. Morning dawned dull, rainy and cold, typical autumn weather the like of which the Luftwaffe would use to full advantage. In addition to the large raids on the capital and other cities, this was also a period of hit and run raids carried out by lone aircraft designed to inflict major damage before turning and fleeing back to France under cloud cover. During the morning several single-engined enemy aircraft had crossed the coast at Harwich and penetrated inland to Birmingham and the surrounding area.

In the city work was carrying on as usual with the early morning rush hour bringing thousands of workers in from the smaller towns. With just a few alerts since the war began, the citizens felt they were secure from any major attack. One particular factory, the Mining and Engineering Company Ltd, known locally as Meco, was engaged in making various components for the military. Originally manu-facturing material purely for the mining industry, they had been contracted to produce parts for the ever increasing number of barrage balloons that were being hoisted aloft around the major cities. The office staff clocked on at 8.30 am and the main factory workforce had been at their benches since early morning. This period remained quiet with no alerts or sirens until midday.

With the office staff taking their lunch break at 12.15, the main workforce were still on the shop floor waiting for the 12.30 hooter to signal their lunch hour. Suddenly, without any warning or sirens, a lone Ju 88 flew low over the Cinderella Shoe Factory and Alley and MacLellan Ltd in Bromyard Road. People stopped in the streets and looked up as the unusual sound of an aircraft so low caught their attention. Seeing the Balkan Cross and the Swastikas as they had never seen them before, many began to run for shelter.

With its bomb doors open, the Ju 88 approached the Meco works at around 300 ft. The local Home Guard, part of the factory workforce, who were outside at the time, grabbed their ancient rifles and pistols in an attempt to fire at the raider. They and many others saw the bombs leave the aircraft. One dropped through the roof of the assembly shop and continued to travel through a brick wall before exploding outside the Meco building amongst some houses in Happy Land West. The other bomb missed the works but exploded in Lambert Road,

War work in an engineering shop in Hereford.
(Maureen Beauchamp via D.Foxton)

A house damaged in the raid on the Meco works. (Worcester Record Office)

demolishing several houses. Of the two bombs dropped, the one that actually hit the factory did so at an angle causing it to continue travelling through the building. It demolished the canteen which 15 minutes later would have been packed with people. As it was, seven men died with three other people seriously injured including a canteen attendant, Doris Tindall. Sixty others suffered minor wounds. The second bomb missed the factory by the narrowest of margins, hit the concrete paving outside and exploded, bringing down several houses in the process.

Having dropped his bombs the enemy aircraft then proceeded to machine-gun the street. People, screaming and terrified, ran for whatever cover they could find. As the Ju 88 roared overhead, the Home Guard continued to fire at it with small arms. Whether any of their bullets registered is debatable as the same aircraft later flew over the Bromyard Road, continuing to fire its machine guns.

The ARP, ambulances and fire tenders were soon on the scene as a cordon was placed around the factory. Clearance work began immediately but with the factory working a 24-hour shift pattern, the men and women were feeling the effects of constant work with no breaks. It had been intended that the weekend following would be a rest weekend but in the event it became the busiest as everyone gave their time to clear the rubble and allow a limited amount of work to continue. By the Sunday much of the wreckage had been cleared and with temporary buildings filling the role of the permanent ones and a large tarpaulin covering the hole in the roof, production was able to start the following Tuesday. Maybe a telegram that was received from Lord Beaverbrook, the Minister of Aircraft Production, shortly after the attack spurred the workforce on. It read: 'WIRE BACK FULL PARTICULARS DEATHS AND INJURIES – MAXIMUM EXTENT OF DAMAGE AND ESTIMATED EARLIEST DATE OF CONTINUATION AND PRODUCTION'!

Edward Dodsworth vividly remembers Worcester's worst moment: 'although only very young I remember this day well. As a five-year-old I had just left my kindergarten school, Trethill in Comer Road and was standing at a bus stop outside the school with my mum. It was about midday. I heard an aircraft and looked up to see a German bomber, the markings on the wings were very clear and it was quite low. It dropped two bombs on the Meco works about a half mile from where I stood. Seven men were killed and over sixty injured. The school I attended was in the grounds of a local GP, Dr Galbraith. Someone from his house came out into the road, and ushered us all into an air raid shelter in their garden. This was quite an experience for a five-year-old! Bombs also fell in Hindlip, Tunnel Hill, Brookend Farm, Kempsey and Bennett's Farm, Lower Wick. Though exciting at the time, on reflection it caused a lot of people a lot of heartache.'

Surprisingly, Worcester's nine-centuries-old Cathedral was spared any damage from German bombs. Costly measures, however, were taken to protect the Cathedral's priceless monuments such as King John's Tomb and Prince Arthur's Chantry, the last resting place of the 15-year-old heir of Henry VII, who died at Ludlow Castle. An extract from the Friends' report of 1942 reads: 'Warned by the so-called *Baedeker* raids on other Cathedral cities, the Dean and Chapter have taken further precautions. The most precious of the historic manuscripts have been stored with those of the British Museum and a complete series of nearly 300 photographs of the monuments and architectural details of the Cathedral have been prepared. Alas, all the iron railings around the Cathedral grounds have been removed and taken away to be melted down for wartime munitions.' A report of the

Bomb damage in Worcester. These houses suffered in the raid on the Meco works. (Worcester Record Office)

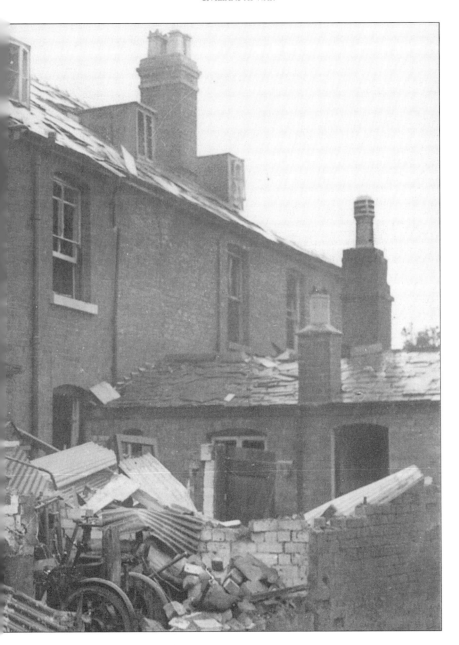

A 'posed' photograph of a Stuka Ju 87 releasing its bombs. (Imperial War Museum)

then Dean, the Very Reverend Arthur Davies, reveals that in July 1944 the Cathedral became the temporary refuge of a large group of women and children evacuated from London where the VI bombs were now falling. It was not until the close of 1944 with the end of the war in sight that the sandbags were finally removed from the monuments and the Cathedral was able to return to its former glory.

The county's other claim to wartime fame was that if the worst had occurred, the control of the war by the government would have been moved to Worcester. The Chief Constable of Worcestershire, Lloyd Williamson, MC, would have been required by the Cabinet Office to make Hindlip Hall, Bevere House and Spetchley available at a minute's notice. It was also rumoured that the King and Queen would be going to Madresfield Court, where they would have been neighbours to Queen Wilhelmena of Holland at nearby Croome Court. There were plans to move the Admiralty to Malvern School where the science block would have become the central signal station for Britain's battle fleet.

By July 1943, Worcestershire had been hit by 778 HE bombs together with 8,077 incendiaries. Despite attacks and incidents in both counties, Middle England was still considered a relatively safe place. Bearing this enviable position in mind, 14 US military hospitals were hurriedly built to adminster aid to injured GIs from the battlefields of Europe and North Africa. In Herefordshire there were two at Kington, two at Foxley near Hereford and one at Leominster. Worcestershire saw five hospitals built at Malvern Wells, one at Wolverley near Kidderminster, two at Burlish near Stourport and one at Bromsgrove. The hospital locations were served by a rail link which came from Southampton where injured soldiers were disembarked from troop ships. The main lines of the London, Midland & Scottish and Great Western railway routes terminated at Great Malvern, Hereford and Worcester. From these stations the link ran to every hospital in the area. The entire network of hospitals came under the control of the 12th Medical Hospital Centre whose headquarters was at Malvern Link.

Victory at last. Servicewomen celebrate with Americans in Worcester.

The D-Day landings saw the hospitals reach their peak with 16,835 wounded GIs receiving treatment between June and December 1944. Overall, 79,000 wounded American servicemen received treatment at the hospitals, all of which luckily remained untouched by enemy bombing.

One of the less-known aspects of the hospitals was that several airstrips within the area were used to fly in injured men, mainly in Stinson L-5 Sentinels and Piper L-4 Cub aircraft. Colwall was used for the army hospitals grouped around the Malvern area, while at Hanbury the aircraft were connected to a large Army camp at Droitwich. Two strips are known to have existed at Kidderminster. One was at Stone and used by British Westland Lysanders whilst the other was American, situated at Wolverley Hospital and Camp. Madresfield was a US Army strip near Malvern, and it is believed that US Army aircraft used the gravel drive to the main house at Westwood Park as a landing strip.

The later years of the war saw very little enemy action over the two counties. The return to peace in 1945 brought a complete change in the pattern of life. Herefordshire and Worcestershire, like every county in the land, had to adapt to a new beginning. Some of the wartime buildings still exist, now put to more peaceful uses. The memories and scars, however, of 'the civilians' war' would remain for generations to come.

HAD WE LOST THE WAR

'As soon as we beat England we shall make an end of you Englishmen once and for all. Able-bodied men and women between the ages of 16 and 45 will be exported as slaves to the Continent. The old and weak will be exterminated.

'All men remaining in Britain as slaves will be sterilised, a million or two of the young women of the Nordic type will be segregated in a number of stud farms where, with the assistance of picked German sires, during a period of ten to twelve years they will produce annually a series of Nordic infants to be brought up in every way as Germans.

'These infants will form the future population of Britain. They will be partially educated in Germany and only those who fully satisfy the Nazis' requirements will be allowed to return to Britain and take up permanent residence. The rest will be sterilised and sent to join slave gangs in Germany. Thus, in a generation or two, the British will disappear.'

These are the chilling words spoken by SS-Obergruppenfuhrer Richard Walter Darre, one of the Nazis' ideologists. We must never forget the sacrifice that saved us all from such a fate.

BIBLIOGRAPHY

During my research I consulted many books. I list them below with grateful thanks to the authors.

Wings over the Wye, Philip Hughes (self-published, 1984)

RAF Pershore – A History, Glyn Warren (self-published, 1982)

The Narrow Margin, D. Wood and D. Dempster (Hutchinson, 1961)

Wartime Worcestershire, Jeff Carpenter (self-published, 1982)

Worcestershire at War, Glyn Warren (self-published, 1983)

Winning the Radar War, J Nissen with A.W. Cockerill (Robert Hale, 1989)

Britain's Military Airfields, D.J. Smith (Patrick Stephens, 1989)

Aircraft of the RAF since 1918, Owen Thetford (Putnam, 1957)

Bomber Command War Diaries, M. Middlebrook and C. Everitt (Viking, 1985)

Go To It, 6th Airborne Division, Peter Harclerode (Catton Editions, 1990)

Angry Skies across the Vale, Brian Kedward (self-published)

Pathfinder, AVM D.C.T. Bennett, CBE, DSO (Goodall, 1988)

The Life and Works of Alan Dower Blumlein, Robert Charles Alexander (Focal Press, 1999)

Fields of Deception, Colin Dobinson, (Methuen, 2000)

Battle of Britain Then and Now, Winston G. Ramsey (After the Battle, 1980)

The Berlin Raids, Martin Middlebrook (Viking, 1988)

Warwickshire Airfields in the Second World War, Graham Smith (Countryside Books, 2004)

Angriff Westland, Dillip Sarkar (Sutton Publishing, 2000)

The Blitz – Volume 2, Winston G. Ramsey (After the Battle, 1999)

Together We Fly, SMM (Geoffrey Bles, 1940)

Allied Photo Reconnaissance, Chris Staerck (Parkgate, 1998)

The Royal Air Force, Michael Armitage (Cassell, 1993)

The Spirit of Wartime, Unknown (1995)

Aircraft of World War Two, K.G. Munson (Ian Allan, 1982)

INDEX

RAF SQUADRONS & UNITS TO 1945